A HISTORY OF STRATEGY

CASTALIA HOUSE

A HISTORY OF STRATEGY
From Sun Tzu to William S. Lind

MARTIN VAN CREVELD

A History of Strategy: From Sun Tzu to William S. Lind

by Martin van Creveld

Published by Castalia House
Kouvola, Finland
www.castaliahouse.com

First published as *The Art of War: War and Military Thought* by Cassell
(2000)

Editor: Vox Day
Cover Design: Christopher Kallini
Cover Image: *Vive L'Empereur*, Édouard Detaille (1891)

Everything in war is simple, but even the simplest things are complicated.

—Carl von Clausewitz

Contents

FOREWORD

MARTIN van Creveld ranks high among military historians, and given the changes in technology since Napoleonic times, his work is a necessary supplement to Clausewitz. His reflections have influenced strategists and grand tacticians since his first books appeared, and as an Israeli historian he has been in a unique position to observe the changing nature of modern warfare on both the grand strategic and tactical levels, particularly with regards to asymmetric warfare. Scholars and military planners ignore his thoughts at their peril.

I don't entirely agree with him on the effectiveness of guerilla operations absent a sanctuary, or with his conclusions concerning Viet Nam, which I consider to be a victory won, then given up. And while the Iraq War was certainly unwise, I don't believe that it was necessarily unwinnable, as the U.S. military was given an impossible mission, then undermined by political errors made above their pay grade. That being said, if winning is defined as a nation being better off after the war than it was before, it is hard to see how winning in Iraq was ever possible. So perhaps we agree after all.

But whatever your position on modern conflicts might be, Martin van Creveld's writings are worth reading and they are vital to reaching informed conclusions about the art of war.

Jerry Pournelle
Studio City, California

Introduction

THE origins of military thought are unknown. Since war is among the oldest of human activities, and long antedates the invention of writing, the earliest attempts to think it out have not survived. Presumably they took the form of poems which were sung or recited on suitable occasions. We do in fact know that many tribal societies have warlike songs. Composed by anonymous bards and often modified to fit subsequent events as they unfold, their purpose is to record glorious deeds that took place in the past, encourage the warriors on one's own side, and frighten the enemy. And indeed the Homeric poems, like broadly similar ones in other cultures, appear to have originated in just such a collection of songs.

However insightful and however inspiring, poems do not military theory make. This volume, concentrating on systematic attempts to understand the nature of war and the ways in which it should be fought, will present the reader with a brief survey of the development of military theory from its origins to the present day. In doing so I have decided to prefer width over depth. The objective is not so much to analyze a few "great" writers—each of whom has been discussed many times—as to aim at a measure of comprehensiveness. Above all, I want to show the continuity of historical thought concerning the subject of war. Even so, given the very limited space available, some concessions had to be made. Obviously only a small selection of those who have turned their minds to the study of war could be included. The rest, particularly the vast number who have done so since 1945, will have to excuse me if I allow their writings to speak for themselves.

In this connection, the vexed question as to whether and how theory influenced action will be largely put aside. In a conference I once attended, one speaker claimed that World War II American "decision makers"—meaning senior civil servants and generals with research money to spend—treated the social scientists from whom they deigned to commission studies "as dogs treat lampposts." Later it turned out that one of the scientists in question happened to be named Ruth Benedict. Ms. Benedict did not know Japanese, nor had she ever been to Japan. Her study of Japanese culture, written in 1943 and later published under the title *The Chrysanthemum and the Sword*, may or may not actually have influenced any particular decision made during the War. In fact it would be very hard to tell. More important, though, having sold by the hundreds of thousands, it did more to shape Western, American in particular, notions about Japan than almost any other work before or since. Certainly more than the vast majority of "decision makers" whose very names, moderately well known in their own time, have since been forgotten. Many of them would probably have been unable to put whatever ideas they had about Japan in coherent form even if they had tried.

The outline of the volume is as follows. Chapter 1 deals with the ancient Chinese military thinkers. Chapter 2 presents a brief outline of classical, Byzantine, and Western medieval military thought. Chapter 3 covers the period between 1500 and the end of the Seven Years War; Chapter 4, the immediate forerunners of Jomini and Clausewitz as well as those writers themselves. Chapter 5 discusses the rest of the nineteenth century up to 1914. Chapter 6 focuses on Mahan and Corbett as the only two writers on the theory of naval warfare (not to be confused with its history, on which there are many fine works) who are worth studying.

Chapter 7 analyzes the period between the World Wars, including air warfare, armored warfare, the indirect approach, and total warfare. Finally, Chapter 8 outlines some of the debates about war that have taken place since 1945. Doing so, it focuses on nuclear strategy on the one hand and terrorism/guerrilla/insurgency on the other.

The plan for the original volume (*The Art of War: War and Military Thought*, Cassell, 2000) was conceived in consultation with the general editor, my late friend Mr. John Keegan, and the publishing director at Weidenfeld and Nicolson, Ms. Judith Flanders. In accord with them, I decided to keep it free of references so as to retain as much as possible of the limited space available for the text proper. Still the reader who is interested in pursuing the topic further will find a list of readings at the back. In this way, it is to be hoped, the demands of both brevity and scholarship can be reconciled.

1. Chinese Military Thought

As indicated in the introduction, the earliest known writings on the subject of war did not constitute theoretical treatises. Instead they took the form of narratives; poems that had been put down such as the Epic of Gilgamesh and the Homeric poems, or prose accounts commemorating individual campaigns and battles such as may be found inscribed on ancient Egyptian, Babylonian, and Assyrian monuments. Both the prose accounts and the poems were intended to record and glorify events which may or may not have taken place, but which, even in the case of the Epic of Gilgamesh with its array of gods and god-like heroes, may have contained some kernel of truth. In addition, the poems in particular served the purpose of inspiring the young to deeds of excellence.

In China, which is where our survey must start, a third type of writing on war developed and enjoyed prominence. China after the fall of the Chou (ca. 400 BC) was divided into a large number of warring principalities. Fighting each other tooth and nail, these principalities developed standing professional armies as well as expert generals. Between about 400 and 200 BC several of these generals appear to have put their methods down in writing. There were also various texts which were written by others and attributed to them by way of enhancing those texts' authority.

In some cases, including that of Sun Tzu, the greatest of their number, the generals may not have been historical figures, but rather legendary pegs upon which anonymous authors hung their own thoughts. This method is still often used in China today. To make one's case, one does not stress one's originality as a modern Westerner would do. On the contrary, one attributes what one is saying to someone who lived long ago and whose fame is greater than one's own.

Once composed or written, both martial poems and prose accounts of war constituted public possessions. They were recited, read, or even inscribed on stone. Not so the Chinese texts. Precisely because they claimed to lay bare the methods which famous generals used in order to gain their victories, these military manuscripts were treated as state secrets. Their nature is evident from their names: e.g. "T'ai Kung's Six Secret Teachings," "The Methods of the Ssu-ma," "Three Strategies of Huang Shihkung" and the "Military Methods" attributed to Sun Pin. All these, as well as several others, were products of the period of the warring principalities. They tended to disappear into royal archives where they were only made available to the elect. Given that they were written on strips of bamboo and joined together by having strings passed through holes in them, there was plenty of occasion for them to fall into disorder over time. Only during medieval (Sung) times were seven of the surviving texts copied or printed on silk and disseminated, serving as textbooks on which the annual military examinations were based. One, by Sun Pin, disappeared altogether. It only came back to light in 1972 when a Han tomb was opened and a copy discovered.

Some of the texts that have come down to us are presented in the form of lectures given by commanders to the rulers whose forces they commanded. Or, in some cases, sought to command. For example, in Wu Tzu's address to the Marquis of Wei, he is described as having given his exposition over a glass of wine, while seated on a mat. Other texts consist of short, pungent phrases which had been stated by, or attributed to, some outstanding general and were then surrounded by the comments of others who expanded on his words, or illustrated them by the use of historical examples. In other cases, we can see a discussion unfolding as a ruler, by way of testing his would-be general, presents him with increasingly difficult questions to answer. The more of the material one reads, the more one feels that not all of it is meant to be taken seriously; some of it exhibits a rather playful character as questions, examples and attributions are piled on top of each other to comprise regular mental battles. To help the student keep the essentials in mind mnemonic devices are often employed, e.g. "the five principles," "the six preservations," "the nine maneuvers," and the like.

Finally, the texts in question cannot be understood without bearing in mind the underlying way in which Chinese culture approaches war. War was neither a means in the hands of policy nor an end in itself. Instead it was regarded as an evil; albeit one that was sometimes made necessary by the imperfection of the world. "Weapons are instruments of ill omen" said Sun Tzu, the oldest and most famous general of all who may or may not have been a historical figure. "However vast the state, he who takes pleasure in the military will perish" added Sun Pin, reputed to have lived a century or so after Sun Tzu and to have been the latter's direct descendant. As Wu Tzu told the Marquis of Wei in their first interview, "a ruler might not have a liking for military affairs. Still not to prepare for war was to fail in his duty—when the dead lie stiff and you grieve for them, you have not attained righteousness." "War is of vital importance for the state," said Sun Tzu. Therefore, "military affairs cannot be but investigated," Sun Pin concluded.

To the Chinese, war was both a necessary evil and a temporary departure from "cosmic harmony," or *dao*. By definition, *dao* can only be restored by *dao*. Hence the war will be won by the side possessing the greatest Virtue, Virtue itself being but another translation of *dao*. "You should cultivate your Virtue ... and observe the *dao* of Heaven" says Ta'i Kung in his Opening Instructions. "In general, warfare is a question of Heaven, material resources, and excellence," says Ssu-ma Ch'ien. "Appraise it [war] in terms of the five fundamental factors," says Sun Tzu. "The first of these factors is moral influence ... by moral influence I mean that which causes the people to be in harmony with their leaders, so that they will accompany them in life and unto death without fear of mortal peril." In the words of Sun Pin, "engaging in a battle without righteousness, no one under Heaven would be able to be solid and strong."

The military virtue of an army takes the form of strict discipline. Or perhaps one should say that, since necessity is not for every private to judge, discipline is the general's way to impose it on his troops. A famous story told about Sun Tzu illustrates the point. As Sun Tzu asked the King of Wu to employ him as a general, the king in turn asked him if he could fashion an army out of the royal wives and concubines. Sun Tzu said he could, and promptly set about to teach them drill. The women took it as a lark: laughing and joking among themselves, they disobeyed Sun Tzu's instructions. Having explained himself several times over, and seeing himself disobeyed still, he ordered that the king's two favorite wives be executed. To the king, who tried to intervene, Sun Tzu explained that since he himself was now the commanding general he need not take all the sovereign's orders. After the two had been executed the remainder immediately fell into line and carried out the required evolutions. Putting himself at their head, Sun Tzu told the king that they would now be prepared to follow his orders "through fire and water."

The need for strict discipline as a basis for all military action is equally evident in the remaining texts. According to Ssu-Ma the perfect army, placed far in the legendary past, requires neither rewards nor punishments. To make use of rewards but impose no punishments is the height of instruction; to impose punishments but issue no rewards is the height of awesomeness. Finally, employing a mixture of both punishments and rewards—combining sticks with carrots, as modern terminology has it—will end up by causing Virtue to decline. Thus the basic idea of *dao*, which underlines every one of these texts, breaks through once again. Governed by necessity, the best-disciplined army is so flawless that it requires neither rewards nor punishments. Behaving as if it were a single personality, it will follow its commander of its own accord. However, as the remaining texts make clear, this is an ideal that is rarely, if ever, attained.

These matters having been seen to, one may discuss such questions as organization, armaments, and supply. To Wei Liao Tzu, organization was primarily a question of establishing clear regulations so that every soldier would know just what was expected of him. The men (he also speaks of chariots, though by the age of the warring states they were obsolete) were to be divided into units five, ten, one hundred, one thousand, and ten thousand strong, each with its own commander. In each unit, the strongest and most outstanding soldiers were to be positioned in front.

According to T'ai Kung, the commander in chief was to surround himself by: 1. A chief of planning. 2. Five planning officers. 3. Three astrologers. 4. Three topographers. 5. Nine "strategists" (what we would call staff officers), "responsible for discussing divergent views, analyzing the probable success or failure of various operations"). 6. Four supply officers. 7. A variety of officers responsible for keeping discipline, gathering intelligence, carrying out engineering jobs, administering medicines, and accounting. Command was exercised by using pennants, gongs, drums, and whistles. The pennants were to be employed by day, the other three by night.

All the texts under consideration are set in a legendary past, assumed to be both unchanging and far superior to the present. Hence they have relatively little to say about armament. In this respect they differ sharply from the voluminous discussions of our present-day, so-called "Revolution in Military Affairs" which are based on the assumption that the key to warfare is shaped by technology. In the China of the warring principalities, a revolution in military affairs had already taken place. Cavalry was taking the place of chariots. The use of large formations of infantry was on the rise, iron weapons had replaced bronze, and swords had supplanted daggers.

In his chapter on "Preparation of Strategic Power," Sun Pin gives a succinct account of the evolution of weapons and equipment as well as their use. "The Yellow Emperor created swords and imagized military formations upon them. Yi created bows and crossbows and imagized strategic power on them. Yu created boats and carts and imagized (tactical) changes on them. T'ang and Wu [all these are legendary emperors] made long [i.e. missile] weapons and imagized the strategic imbalance of power on them." Thus four types of weapons and equipment are listed. The first provides formations with staying power. The second enables users to act from a distance. The third provides mobility (change); and the fourth enables them to dominate the enemy. The art of war consists of combining the four, employing each in correct interaction with the others so as to bring out their advantages and mask their weaknesses. "If one knows their *dao* then the army will be successful … if someone wants to employ them but does not know their *dao*, the army will lack success."

Concerning supply, "money is the sinews of war." According to Sun Tzu, an army numbering one hundred thousand men with all its equipment, if led one thousand *li* into enemy territory, will cost one thousand gold coins a day to maintain. Included in the calculus are such esoteric items as presents for the commanders' guests and glue for fixing broken chariots. However, the greatest expenditure is that which must cover provisioning. The larger the distance from home, the more ruinous the cost of transport. For that reason, but also because the presence of an army will cause the price of everything to rise, a commander who tries to support his forces from his own country will ruin the people. It is therefore best to impose the logistic burden on the enemy, a principle that Sun Tzu considers so important that he repeats it twice.

T'ai Kung, whom we have already quoted, wanted the army to have four officers who would look after the organization of supply. They are "responsible for calculating the requirements for food and water; preparing the food stocks and supplies and transporting the provisions along the route; and supplying the five grains so as to ensure that the army will not suffer any hardship or shortage." Once an army had entered enemy country it was to resort to requisitioning as a matter of course. Conversely an army operating in a country where there were neither towns nor villages to feed the men nor grass to meet the needs of horses and oxen found itself in dire straits. In such a situation, continues T'ai Kung, the commander should "seek some opportunity to trick the enemy and quickly get away." If necessary, by using "gold and jade" to obtain the necessary intelligence.

Plentiful supplies, everything that is needed by way of arms and equipment, good organization, and strict discipline constitute the foundation on which a successful campaign can be built. Provided these are available, it is time to carry out a survey as to the respective strength of one's own side and that of the enemy. The favor of Heaven apart, four factors are to be considered. They are, first the weather, second terrain, third command, and fourth doctrine. The weather will determine which season is the most favorable for campaigning and how this is to be done. Knowledge of the terrain will enable the general to calculate the size of the forces, the kind of troops needed, and which kind of operational plan to adopt. Command refers to the qualities of the opposing general; whereas by doctrine is meant everything that pertains to the organization of the enemy and his supply system. "There is," sums up Sun Tzu, "no general who has not heard of these … matters. Those who master them, win; those who do not, are defeated."

But how, precisely, will victory be won? Since violence represents a disturbance of *dao*, its use should be kept to the indispensable minimum. "No state has ever benefited from a long war" said Sun Tzu. "Those that garner five victories will meet with disaster; those with four victories will be exhausted; those with three victories will become hegemons; those with two victories will be kings; and those with one victory will become emperors" (Wu Tzu). The best way to settle a dispute, explains Sun Tzu, is by diplomacy as when you negotiate with the enemy and give him presents. Second best is the use of dirty tricks such as assassinating the enemy commander or bribing his officers. Those who cannot use dirty tricks engage in maneuver. Those who cannot maneuver fight a battle, and those who cannot fight a battle lay siege.

In Clausewitz's view, "the maximum employment of force by no way rules out the use of intelligence." Not so the Chinese commander-sages who, following the fundamental worldview laid down by Lao Tzu, look at the two as opposites. They always seek to minimize the first by relying on the second. Force is to be used in carefully measured doses, neither more nor less than is necessary and in sharp, short bursts. This means that it must be very precisely aimed. "Throw rocks at eggs" is how Sun Tzu puts it in one of those incomparable metaphors that have helped make his work the most famous of all. When you are strong, pretend to be weak so as to tempt the enemy. When you are weak, pretend to be strong so as to deter him. Use speed and secrecy to make out that you concentrate at one place, then attack at another. If weaker than the enemy, avoid him, harass him, and draw him into terrain that is unfavorable for him; if equal to him, wait patiently until he commits an error, as in chess. Confuse him and keep him ignorant of your designs by offering bait, mounting feints, and/or spreading disinformation as appropriate. Finally, when you have the enemy where you want him—i.e. just when he feels secure—fall on him like a thunderbolt.

Thus the strongest, most successful action is at the same time the most economic one. To achieve this ideal, two things are needed. The first is extreme flexibility which will enable one to take advantage of fleeting opportunities. Said Sun Tzu, "an army is like water which adapts itself to the configuration of the ground." Plans must have many branches and be so arranged that alternate ones can be put into operation without undue disruption. Forces earmarked for one mission must be capable of switching to another, if necessary, at a moment's notice, and without either commanders or troops missing a beat. In all this activity there can be no fixed routine, no unalterable modus operandi, but as many stratagems as there are enemies and circumstances.

The second requirement is intelligence. Still remaining with Sun Tzu, he distinguishes between five types of spies. To wit, local spies, internal spies, turned spies, dead spies, and the living spy. Local spies are simply travelers and residents of the theater of war who are examined concerning the terrain, its resources, and whatever they may know of the enemy. Internal spies are people who hold positions inside the enemy's forces. Turned spies are double agents, i.e. the enemy's spies who have been forced or persuaded to work for us. Dead [expendable] spies are sent out to the enemy camp in order to spread disinformation. Finally, living spies consist of our own agents who are sent out in the expectation that they will return and deliver their reports. The entire question of espionage requires "the wisdom of a sage" both when it comes to perceiving the truth of incoming reports and in handling those valuable but difficult creatures, the spies themselves. "There are no areas in which one does not employ spies."

Correctly and systematically employed, espionage will endow the commander with a thorough understanding of the enemy, his strengths and weaknesses. The art of war demands that the former be avoided and the latter, exploited. In other words, that the enemy's qualities be made to mesh, or synchronize, with our own. Thus knowing oneself is no less, and may be more, of a requirement than understanding the enemy. According to T'ai tsung, "know them and know yourself" is the great essence of military strategy. "Contemporary generals, even if they do not know the enemy, ought to be able to know themselves, so how could they lose the advantage?" Said Sun Tzu: "Know the enemy and know yourself. In a hundred battles you will never be in peril. When you are ignorant of the enemy but know yourself, your chances of winning or losing are equal. If ignorant both of your enemy and of yourself, you are certain in every battle to be in peril." To which the commentator Li Chu'an adds: 'such people are called "mad bandits." What can they expect if not defeat?'

In spite of their antiquarian bent, which leads to the discussion of out of date weapons and sometimes gives the whole a quaint air, for sheer sophistication the Chinese military writings have never been equaled. In them high seriousness alternates with play, pungent sayings with relaxed discussion, abstract analysis with an abundance of concrete examples taken from the annals of the warring states and more often than not associated with the names of famous generals. Yet seldom do they descend to the kind of technical trivia which, as we shall presently see, marks much of ancient Western military thought. An underlying humanity pervades all: "[virtue is] sparing the people from death, eliminating the hardships of the people, relieving the misfortunes of the people, and sustaining the people in their extremities" (T'ai Kung). This is combined with a readiness to ignore personal considerations concerning love and hate, take the most drastic measures (including such as we should consider underhand or immoral), and inflict the harshest punishments. All as may be dictated by necessity which knows no bounds. Above all, no clear line is drawn between military affairs and the rest of life. On the contrary, it is a question of achieving *dao* in the military field also.

As in the rest of life, the best way to achieve *dao* is not to depart from it in the first place. To paraphrase, the best war is that which is never fought. The second best is that which is avoided, the third that which is won without bloodshed, the fourth that which involves heavy loss of life. The fifth is that which has to be repeated time after time—think of Israel in Gaza! As in Plato's *Republic*, which was written at approximately the same time and where the state is made to stand as a metaphor for the human soul, all five ways of behavior apply not just to the ruler but to the private individual too.

The first marks the way of the commander in chief who is also a sage; the last, that of the man who is both brutal and stupid. Yet praiseworthy as an inclination towards peace may be, on no account should it lead to a neglect of military affairs. "Those who forget warfare will inevitably be endangered" (T'ai tsung). Perhaps it is impossible to do better than to sum up in the words of Lao Tzu, "the Old Master." While not a military expert, he was the father of Daoism and thus stands at the root of every one of the texts we have discussed:

> Once grasp the great form without a form
> and you will roam where you will
> with no evil to fear,
> calm, peaceful, at ease.
> The hub of wheel runs upon the axle.
> In a jar, it is the hole that holds water.
> So advantage is had
> From whatever there is;
> but usefulness rises
> from whatever is not.

2. FROM ANTIQUITY TO THE MIDDLE AGES

W HEN it comes to the writing of military history, classical antiquity has never been surpassed. Thucydides and Sallust and Caesar and Josephus; in the entire record of mankind one looks in vain for authors better capable of describing the goals of commanders, the activities of armies, the motivations of troops, the possibilities and limitations of weapons, and the sufferings of civilians. Not quite on the same level, but still very impressive, are the works of Herodotus, Xenophon, Polybius, and Livy (although from the Renaissance to the Enlightenment it was usually the last-named who was regarded as the greatest historian of all). Both Herodotus and Livy wrote patriotic history and are perhaps a trifle too inclined towards the legendary, the supernatural and the moralistic to suit our supposedly "scientific" taste. Xenophon, though a competent commander and a superb journalist, does not have psychological depth. Polybius represents the point of view of the Hellenistic magistrate and diplomat. As such he certainly knew his business but tends to be dry and technical.

Against this grand tradition *in historicis*, it is remarkable that ancient military theory does not attain nearly the same level of excellence. Certainly this is not due to the absence of great generals. Who in the whole of history can equal an Alexander, a Hannibal, a Scipio, or a Caesar? Yet with the exception of the last-named in his *commentarii*, which are exactly what they claim to be, none of them has left us a firsthand record of his experiences, much less tried to develop them into a systematic treatise on the art of war. Such treatises as do exist, and there are quite a few, were written by decidedly second rate figures. Like their Chinese counterparts most, though probably not all, had some personal experience of war. Unlike their Chinese counterparts, none appears to have commanded at the highest level, let alone acquired fame as a general.

Disregarding Xenophon, whose *Cyropaedia* constitutes not so much military analysis as a semi-imaginary tale concerning the ways of a successful prince, the earliest writer whose work is extant is Aeneas the Tactician in the fourth century BC. The last one is Vegetius who must have written at the very end of the fourth century AD. Judging by the examples which he does and does not adduce, Aeneas wrote before either Philip or Alexander the Great appeared on the scene and transformed Greek warfare. By contrast, Vegetius belongs to the period when the Roman Empire was being metamorphosed into the Byzantine one. Perhaps the fact that they are separated by a gap of almost seven centuries explains why these writers, in contrast with their Chinese opposite numbers, neither possess a common ideology nor adhere to a single world view.

We shall begin with Aeneas. He was the author of a number of treatises on the art of war, all but one of which have been lost. The surviving one deals with a single, highly technical, question: namely, how to defend a besieged city against attack. Chapter 1 deals with the disposition of troops and the preparation of positions. Chapter 2 explains how morale is to be maintained and attempts at treachery and revolution thwarted. In Greek city-states, which, at the time when Aeneas wrote were often threatened by factional strife even as the enemy was at the gates, this was an extremely important question. Chapter 3 explains how sudden raids ought to be foiled. Chapter 4 deals with keeping the enemy away from the walls, chapter 5 with methods for guarding the walls, and chapter 6 with how to meet actual assaults upon the walls and repulse them.

All this is done in a competent enough way and often in considerable detail. For example, there are so and so many methods by which a city's gates can be unlocked and which, accordingly, ought to be guarded against by those who bear the responsibility. Similarly, the passwords with which patrols are issued ought to be carefully selected for memorability and recognizability. Sentries should not be allowed to leave their posts before their replacements have arrived. When sawing through the bolt of a gate, pour on oil so as to proceed faster and make less noise. And so forth and so forth down to the suggestion that, to make a few soldiers appear like many, they should be made to march in lines abreast with each successive rank carrying their spears on alternate shoulders.

In military science as in so many others, attention to detail is absolutely vital. In military science as in so many others, detail on its own does not for genius make. Some of the devices Aeneas suggests, particularly those which deal with encoding methods, appear naïve. Others, such as a kind of optical telegraph for the transmission of messages, were impractical and already subjected to criticism in ancient times. Still, on the whole, his is a useful collection of rules and devices which any competent person appointed to defend a town ought to have at his fingertips. Had our author selected a motto, no doubt it would have been "for want of a nail a city was lost."

As far as can be reconstructed Aeneas's remaining writings dealt with "military preparations," "war finance," "encampments," "plots," "naval tactics," "historical illustrations," and "siege warfare." Supposing them to have been of a similar character to the one which we possess, a person who had mastered them all ought to have had at his disposal a vast depository of somewhat pedestrian military knowledge. It would have come in handy in almost any situation, provided of course sufficient time was available to consult the many volumes in which it was contained. It would not have been of any help at all in the planning of war at the highest level.

No such praise may be bestowed on our next text, Asclepiodotus' *Outline of Tactics*. Asclepiodotus, who flourished around the middle of the first century BC, was a student of the great stoic philosopher Poseidonius. Unlike Aeneas he was not a military man. In fact the treatise itself may have merely been an exercise in rhetoric. At the time the *Tactics* was written, its main subject, i.e. the Greek phalanx, was long out of date and the Roman legion, as used e.g. by Pompey and Julius Caesar, was approaching its zenith. Yet nothing in Asclepiodotus' work indicates that he was living in an age of military genius. Instead, the book takes the original Greek meaning of "tactics," i.e. "order," literally. It contains a rather pedantic discussion of the distances to be kept between the men in the phalanx; the length of their spears; the width of their shields; the titles of the leaders of various sub-formations; and how to make the men turn right or left without falling into disorder. The treatise ends in a long list of orders such as: "stand by to take arms! (*parastethi epi ta hopla*, to give the reader who is not a classicist an idea of what it sounded like); Silence in the ranks! And Attention! Baggage men fall out! Take up arms! Shoulder arms." It is the Greek drillmaster whose voice we hear.

The phalanx apart, Asclepiodotus also includes brief discussions of light infantry (peltasts), cavalry, chariots and elephants. However, they are even less inspiring than the rest. One gets the impression that, by the time he reaches the last two, the author himself, aware that they are hopelessly out of date, can scarcely suppress a yawn. The entire work bears an abstract character, failing as it does to adduce a single example drawn from actual military life. Nor does it even try to discuss the way in which the various kinds of troops ought to interact with each other and the enemy, i.e. tactics as we would understand the term. Still, as one modern author has commented, it is useful to know that there existed a Macedonian, a Laconian, and a Cretan countermarch. Let alone that the last of these was also known as the Persian. Not to forget the earth-shaking fact that the leader of a single elephant was known as an animal commander or *zoarchos* and of two, a beast commander (*therarchos*).

Like Asclepiodotus, whom he followed by about one hundred years, Onasander was primarily a student of philosophy. His work, entitled The General (*Strategikos*), may also have been intended as an exercise in rhetoric. If so, it must be admitted that it is considerably less technical than that of his predecessor. Having dedicated his book "to the Romans, and especially to those of the Romans who have attained senatorial dignity and who through the wisdom of Augustus Caesar [Nero is meant] have been raised to the power of consul or general," he proposes to discuss everything that pertains to the good commander. First things first: the post of commander must be taken by one who is "temperate, self-restrained, vigilant, frugal, hardened to labor, alert, free from avarice, neither too young nor too old, indeed a father of children if possible, a ready speaker, and a man with a good reputation." The bulk of Onasander's first chapter consists of a very sensible explanation as to why each quality is needed.

The rest of the treatise is equally balanced and unexciting. Chapters 2 and 3 (each chapter is no more than a page or so long) describe the character which the subordinate officers must have as well as the need for the commander to have an advisory council of some sort. Chapters 4 and 5 deal with the need to have a reasonable, read not unjust, cause for war as well as the importance of listening to soothsayers and omens. Chapters 6 and 7 deal with the maintenance of military formations and here, too, Onasander's advice is sensible enough. Order should be maintained at all times. Depending on the country in question, i.e. whether it is wide open or narrow, formations should be either broad or deep. The former is better suited for fighting, the latter for marching; other things being equal, some compromise between them should be found. Vulnerable elements of the army, such as its medical equipment, pack animals and baggage should be placed either in the center of the column or, in case the latter comes under attack, on the side that is farthest away from the enemy. Allied country is not be plundered and the question of supply is to be attended to.

Like Asclepiodotus, Onasander does not provide any examples to illustrate or clarify his meaning (though it must be admitted that his meaning is almost always perfectly clear). Unlike Asclepiodotus (and also unlike Aeneas), it is only rarely that his advice degenerates into trivia. The discussion of the way the different arms ought to be arrayed and cooperate with each other points to real insight on his part, albeit that unfortunately the force he has in mind is not the Roman legion of his day but the long obsolete phalanx. Various tactics, such as the feigned retreat, the need to hold some troops in reserve so as to assist formations that have become exhausted, and the effectiveness of sudden attacks directed against the enemy's flank and rear are discussed. All this is done in a sensible if curiously bloodless manner, and again without any illustrations or examples.

Thus far the arrangement of the material is reasonable and orderly. However, from chapter 23 onward it degenerates. As the author begins to jump from one subject to the next without really bothering to maintain any particular order, the text loses all coherence. Still, while scarcely sensational, much of the advice offered continues to be quite sensible. For example, the need for the general to make the troops look after their equipment or to avoid fighting in person. Victorious troops should be justly rewarded, defeated ones encouraged, and cities that have surrendered fairly treated. The dead should be buried and the gods always honored by performing the appropriate rites. In sum, a "good man" who attends to all these "will not only be a brave defender of his fatherland and a competent leader of an army but also, for the permanent protection of his own reputation, will be a sagacious strategist."

In our own day the works of Aeneas, Asclepiodotus and Onasander have long been dead. Understandably so, given the dry, schematic, and sometimes pettifogging way in which they approach their subjects. Not so during the period from about 1450 to 1700 when "the ancients" were revived by humanist scholarship and enjoyed high esteem. Onasander in particular was described as "the most learned, concise and valuable [treatise] to be found upon the art of war" (Francis Guilliman, 1583). That is even more true of the next two authors we must consider, Frontinus and Vegetius. Both of them were not "dead" at all, but reissued and translated and considered to be of immediate practical use to commanders of the Renaissance and beyond.

Sextus Julius Frontinus was a Roman official whose career spanned the last quarter of the first century AD. He accumulated considerable experience, both military—he fought the tribes in modern Wales—and as a civilian in his capacity as supervisor of the city's aqueducts. His main work on the art of war has been lost. What remains is the *Strategemata*, best translated as "tricks of the trade" and apparently meant to serve as a companion to the theoretical treatise. It consists of four books of which the last one was written by another person.

Unlike so many others, the *Strategemata* has nothing to say about raising troops, formations, discipline, etc.. Instead it is divided into fifty chapters with titles such as "Distracting the Attention of the Enemy," "By What Means the Enemy May be Reduced to Want," "On Terrorizing the Besieged," and "On the Effect of Discipline." Each chapter contains a list of devices used by past commanders in the realization of their plans. For example, "whenever Alexander of Macedon had a strong army he chose the sort of warfare in which he could fight in open battle." An ambassador of Scipio Africanus who was conducting a parley once deliberately had a horse run wild in the enemy's camp, presenting his men with an opportunity to chase it around and thus observe more than they should have. The Carthaginians, lacking material for cordage, used their women's hair to equip their fleet. Caesar once spurred his soldiers to battle by showering such praise on his Tenth Legion that the rest became envious and wanted to emulate it.

Since Frontinus makes no attempt to link the various devices with each other, as an exercise in monotony his work has seldom been equaled. Yet it must be conceded that, as long as the technical limitations of his age are borne in mind, many of his suggestions were practical. A commander capable of employing only a small fraction of them would be considered highly inventive. Presumably that explains why he was quite popular in antiquity and remained so throughout the Middle Ages and beyond. When the great scholar Jean Gerson (1363–1429) drew up a list of works which ought to be in the library of the French Dauphin he included Frontinus. Machiavelli, who though a far greater writer possessed a practical mind not so very different from Frontinus' own, considered him indispensable. He continued to be read, and quoted, by commanders down to the third quarter of the eighteenth century.

Writing some three centuries after Frontinus, Flavius Renatus Vegetius and his *Epitoma Rei Militaris* (A Summary of Military Matters) stand in a class all of his own. Vegetius was not a soldier but an administrator in the Imperial service. He appears to have produced the work on behalf of a Roman Emperor by the name of Valentian, though we do not know which one out of two possible candidates he had in mind. Faced with the much weakened state of the Empire, he charged Vegetius with explaining how the "ancient" Romans had gone about their business so successfully. Consequently the *Epitoma* does not deal with the army of Vegetius' own day but with an idealized version of previous ones. Among

the sources mentioned are Cato, Sallust, Frontinus, and the military or-
dinances of Augustus, Trajan, and Hadrian. Thus it is likely that the
military organization Vegetius described never existed at any single time
and place. Still it is a tribute to his work that he succeeded in bringing it
to life and presenting us with a remarkably coherent whole.

Of the four parts, the first one discusses recruits. That includes the
way they were selected ("fishermen, fowlers, confectioners, weavers, and
all those who appear to have been engaged in occupations appropriate to
women should not, in my opinion, be allowed near the barracks") and
trained in marching, the use of arms, and the various formations used
in battle. Part 2 gives the best account of the legion's organization we
have or are likely to have. That includes its organization; the sub-units
of which it consists; the officers; the promotion system; the auxiliary
services; the troop of horse; and the way in which it ought to be drawn
up for battle. Part 3 deals with the various tactical methods the legion
used. Part 4, which seems to have been tagged on by another writer,
discusses fortifications and naval warfare. Yet precisely because Vegetius
does not focus on any particular period his work is as much prescriptive
as it is descriptive. From beginning to end the importance of thorough
training, strong discipline, hard work (as in building a fortified camp each
night), and sound planning are emphasized.

In particular, part 3 ends with a long list of do's and don'ts. For
example, "it is better to have several bodies of reserves than to extend
your front too much;" and "troops are not to be led into battle unless
they are confident of success." The book's succinct style, plus the fact
that it was dedicated to an emperor and thus had a direct link with the
prestige of Imperial Rome, plus the many useful suggestions it contains in
regard to fortification in particular, explain why, for over a thousand years
after it was written, it remained the most popular military handbook of
all. As late as 1770 one Austrian field-marshal, the Prince de Ligne, went

so far as to claim that "Vegetius had been inspired by God." This was true even though, during the Middle Ages, the core of armies almost always consisted of cavalry rather than the infantry of which Vegetius wrote.

Both the *Strategemata* and the *Epitoma* were written in Latin, which is another reason why they were so popular during the European Middle Ages. Not so, of course, the military treatises produced by the Byzantine Empire. The best-known, the *Strategikon*, is attributed to the Emperor Maurice (reigned 582–602). In fact it was composed in his name by others. Written not long after the great campaigns of Belisarius and Narses, it represents Byzantine military practice at its zenith. Part 1, comprising the introduction, describes the training, equipment, and discipline of the *tagma*, a cavalry formation. Parts 2 and 3 deal with the way in which the *tagma* ought to be prepared and positioned for battle. Part 4 advises the commander on how to deal with ambushes and set them up. Part 5 discusses the way baggage trains are to be arrayed, part 6 various tactics and drills to be used when confronting the enemy. The subject of part 7 is "generalship" (*strategia*). Far from dealing with matters of supreme import pertaining to the overall conduct of the campaign, however, it is subtitled "the points with which the general must consider." This includes blessing the flags; organizing the squads; gathering enemy intelligence; making speeches to encourage the troops; interrogating prisoners; punishing offenders; watering the horses; and making sure that the men carry rations in their saddlebags.

A general who has followed the *Strategikon*'s instructions up to this point ought to have his army ready and drawn up for battle. Accordingly part 8 deals with "points to be observed on the day of battle," such as the need for the general not to overburden himself and to conceal his intentions for as long as possible. Part 9 deals with methods for launching surprise attacks, and part 10 with offensive and defensive siege operations including "building a border fortress by stealth and without open battle."

Obviously produced by a group of experts, all this material makes very good sense. And indeed traces of its influence on questions such as castrametation are said to be discernible in the conduct of actual campaigns such as the one against the Arabs in 636 AD.

Even more interesting, both to the historian and probably also to the contemporary commander, is Part 11. It provides brief anthropological analyses of the principal enemies facing the Empire, their weaknesses and their strengths, and suggests ways for dealing with each one. For example, "the Persian nation is wicked, dissembling and servile, but at the same time patriotic and obedient." Seldom bothering to look after their flanks, "they are vulnerable to attacks and encirclements from an outflanking position against the flanks and rear of their formations." They should, if possible, be engaged on "open, smooth, and level terrain … without any swamps, ditches or brush which could break up the [Byzantine] formation." By contrast, "the light-haired races place great value on freedom. They are bold and undaunted in battle; daring and impetuous as they are, they consider any timidity and even a short retreat as a disgrace." However, "they are hurt by suffering and fatigue … [as well as] heat, cold, rain, lack of provisions (especially of wine) and postponement of battle." Therefore, "in warring against them one must avoid engaging in pitched battles, especially in the early stages. But do make use of well-planned ambushes, sneak attacks, and stratagems."

Finally, part 12 of the *Strategikon* deals with infantry, an arm which, by that time, had been relegated to the sidelines. Taken as a whole, the work is a masterpiece of sorts. However, the other Byzantine works on military art which have come down to us—all that remains of a vast literature—are less comprehensive and less informative. The earliest of the lot is an anonymous 6th-century treatise whose main subjects are siege warfare on the one hand and the operations of the cavalry phalanx on the other. Then we have the *Tacticon*, an essay on military organization and battle-arrays attributed to Emperor Leo the Wise (866–912). Though usually mentioned in a single breath with the *Strategikon*, in fact it is much less interesting and less original. It is largely an abbreviation of its predecessor and also contains entire passages lifted straight out of Onasander. The list is completed by two late-ninth century essays. One is said to have been the work of Emperor Nicophorus and deals with skirmishing. The other, which is anonymous, examines the way campaigns should be organized.

All these volumes reflect the workings of a highly sophisticated, articulated armed force with numerous subdivisions and an emphasis on combined arms. As might perhaps be expected from the "Byzantines," all also display a strong penchant for secrecy, flexibility, cunning and guile in order to achieve victory. In this respect they resemble the Chinese classics. However, since war is regarded purely as an instrument in the hands of the emperor the underlying humanitarianism which makes the latter so attractive is entirely absent.

During the time when the Byzantine Empire flourished much of Western Europe had been overrun by Barbarian tribes. Their preferred form of military literature, if that is the term, consisted of the *chansons de geste*. They were narrative songs in which the (usually legendary) exploits of (usually legendary) heroes were celebrated. So, for example, the *Chanson de Roland* as the most famous composition of all; so too many others of varying literary quality. Even later, when the higher classes at any rate ceased being illiterate, the Latin West in spite of its marked warlike qualities did not have either professional soldiers or standing armies. Possibly as a result, it produced remarkably little by the way of military textbooks.

Since Byzantine works only became available after the humanist revival, the most popular treatises by far were Frontinus and Vegetius, as already noted. The latter in particular graced many a princely library of which we are informed, including that of Richard Lionheart. These two were supplemented by a number of others whose subject was not so much military theory and practice as the art of "chivalry" and the rules of war. An outstanding specimen is Honoré Bonet, whose Tree of Battles (*L'arbre des batailles*) was written around 1400. Bonet was a monk and a doctor of law. His professed goal was to help mitigate the evils of war—this was the time of the Hundred Years War—which, as a native of Provence, he could see all around him.

In the introduction he defines war as "a discord or conflict that has arisen on account of certain things displeasing to the human will, to the end that such conflict should be turned into agreement and reason." Next, to determine "whence came jurisdiction" (i.e. the origins of the laws which he cites), he gives a brief historical account of "the four great kingdoms of the past." They are Babylon, Persia, Alexander's, and Rome. The core of the book consists of several hundred questions and answers concerning the things that are and are not permitted. "If a soldier has accepted wages for a year, may he put another man in his place during that period?" "Whether it is lawful to give battle on a feast day." "Whether the holder of a safe-conduct may take with him a man of higher estate than himself." "Whether clerics should pay *taillages* or impositions levied for the purposes of a war" (they should not). "If a baron is a vassal of two lords who are at war with each other, which should he help?" And—remember, this was a time of war between France and England—"whether an English student dwelling at Paris for purposes of study could be imprisoned?"

To those who would understand the mentality of war in the Middle Ages Bonet's work, like that of his self-professed disciple Christine de Pisan, is invaluable. Neither they nor the various chronicles constitute military theory, however. They are mentioned here only by way of an indication of the kind of writings which the period in question produced.

Summing up the present chapter, one may perhaps conclude that such theory did not constitute a strong point either of the Latin Middle Ages or of the ancient world. Ignoring the differences that existed between their own feudal system and the Roman Imperial one, medieval people were content with a small number of Roman texts which had been handed down to them and of which they made use as best they could. The ancient world saw the writing of much superb military history; however, judging by what remains the theoretical treatises which it produced tended to be no more than sensible at best and pedestrian at worst.

As to the Byzantine texts, they formed a world apart. Quite obviously they were written by persons who knew what they were talking about. But they exercised little influence outside a small circle of Imperial generals who may have wanted to know such things as (quoting the one on campaign organization) "how to avoid confusion inside the camp." These generals may have carried them about and used them as the situation demanded.

What is more, and as their arrangement suggests, even the best of the works discussed in the present chapter are little more than handbooks. They make suggestions and proffer advice which may be appropriate to this occasion or that. Taking the formations and armament of their own day more or less for granted, however, they seldom rise above the specifics of time and place. From time to time they go lower still, delving into such questions as the use of heated vinegar for splitting rocks and how to train archers to fire accurately. The fact that some of them were in actual use until 1700 and beyond shows how indebted early modern Europe felt itself to the ancient world—or, conversely, how slow the evolution of warfare was. Unlike the Chinese classics they do not provide a coherent philosophy of war. In the West, the only writer who met that demand was Clausewitz. Before we can examine Clausewitz, however, it is necessary to fill in the gap between about 1500 and the end of the Seven Years War.

3. 1500 TO 1763

MACHIAVELLI's place among the great political scientists of history is secure, and deservedly so. No one who has compared *The Prince* to, say, Erasmus's *Ways of a Christian Prince* can but note the immense gap between them. Though separated by no more than two or three years, the latter is a treatise on morals, the former on power. Machiavelli's insights into the nature of power have rarely been equaled, never surpassed. They remain as fresh today as they were when he put them down in 1513.

In spite of the attempts, made by modern historians, to include Machiavelli among "makers of modern strategy," *The Art of War* does not really amount to a first-class treatise on the subject. Written in 1523, the work is cast in the form of a conversation which took place in a Florentine Garden. The chief character is Fabrizio Colonna, a member of a noble family of that name which had disturbed the peace of Rome for centuries. Like others of his kind, this Fabrizio had served as a mercenary commander under Spain's "Catholic Kings," Ferdinand and Isabel, during their wars in northern Italy. Now he is traveling back to his native Rome and, stopping at Florence, ready to hold forth on his experiences.

During his years in office (1498–1512) Machiavelli himself had been in charge of conducting Florence's war against Pisa. The conflict dragged on and on; to save money, Machiavelli at one point persuaded the *signoria* to supplement the mercenaries which were doing the fighting with the conscripted inhabitants of Florence's own *contado* or countryside. The experiment, which was the subject of much skepticism, worked and Pisa was duly taken. Not long thereafter, however, the same troops scattered to the four winds in front of Emperor Maximilian's hard-bitten *Landsknechte*. As the Medici family, which had been expelled in 1494, returned, Florence's republican government fell. Machiavelli himself was briefly imprisoned and tortured.

Nothing daunted, eight years later Machiavelli put his predilection for conscripts into the mouth of Fabrizio Colonna. The common opinion, which had it that civilians could not be successful soldiers, was wrong. "My Romans" during the Republic (both in this work and in others Machiavelli all but ignored the Imperial period) had been the best soldiers in the world. Since they had consisted of conscripts, so ought others in the "modern" age. Having thus proven the superiority of conscripts to his own satisfaction, Machiavelli proceeds to describe their selection, training, discipline, equipment, marching order, methods of castrametation, and the like. All of this was to be done in the Roman manner, partly as could be culled from Livy but mainly as described by Vegetius, even though Vegetius himself belonged to the late Imperial period rather than to the Republican one which Machiavelli so much admired.

Having shown what good soldiers his imaginary Romans were, Machiavelli draws them up for an equally imaginary battle. They are armed with a mixture of Greek and Roman weapons; since the formations he suggests were hopelessly out of date, to prevent them from being blown to pieces he must first of all pretend that artillery is of little use, even at the risk of having his audience laugh at him. Having done so, he is now in a position where he can dispense some useful advice. "In the midst of battle, to confuse the hostile army, it is necessary to make something happen that will bewilder them, either by announcing some reinforcement that is coming or by showing something that appears like it." "When a general wins, he ought with all speed to follow up his victory." A commander "should never fight a battle if he does not have the advantage, or if he is not compelled by necessity." "The greatest and most important matter that a general should attend to is to have near him faithful men, very skillful in war and prudent, with whom he continually advises." "When either hunger or other natural necessity or human passion has brought your enemy to complete desperation … you ought to avoid battle in so far as is in your power." These and similar pearls of wisdom are provided with plentiful illustrations at the hands of examples, most of them taken from the ancient world. After all, if Minucius Rufus and Acilius Glabrio, "Roman consuls" in 217 and 191 BC respectively, could carry out this or that maneuver, why not we?

Thus three of Machiavelli's key propositions—his underestimation of artillery, his recommendation that pikes be supplemented with swords and bucklers, and his preference for citizen-soldiers over professionals—proved to be dead wrong. The last of these ideas even compelled him to strike some decidedly un-Machiavellian attitudes. So, for example, when he claimed that professional soldiers could not be "good men." A claim which, when put into the mouth of a man who was himself a professional soldier, forced him to turn some strange intellectual somersaults. It also compelled him to pretend that Roman military prowess ended around the time of the Gracchi and devote but little attention to the exploits of a Marius, a Sulla, a Pompey, or a Caesar. Even less attention was paid to other Roman commanders who had the misfortune to live during the Imperial period.

Why Machiavelli's work attained the fame that it did remains a mystery. None of his contemporaries took his advice with regards to conscription. However, they do seem to have appreciated his emphasis on discipline and order. He obviously had a good understanding of the differences among the armies of his day. But his discussion of this topic is of interest only to the kind of military historian who takes the Renaissance as his specialty and wants to know, for example, how the Imperial horse differed from the French and Spanish ones. Many of his concrete suggestions are sensible enough. However, being taken almost entirely from Livy, Frontinus and Vegetius (not knowing Greek, and preferring the Roman legion to the Greek phalanx, he placed much less reliance on the remaining ancient authors) they lack originality.

An underlying philosophy of war may be discerned in Machiavelli's insistence that rich and well-ordered states cannot exist without strong defenses. In *The Prince* he says that "a just war is a necessary war," thus cutting through the Gordian knot formed by endless Medieval discussions of Just War from Saint Augustine to Saint Thomas Aquinas. The reason for including him in these pages is principally because he is there and because in other respects he is a commanding intellectual figure. Like a major general standing in the middle of the road, one must salute him whether one wants to or not.

In truth, much of the remaining military thought produced between Machiavelli and the French Revolution is even less impressive. Why this should be the case is not easy to say. Certainly Gustavus and Turenne, Marlborough and Prince Eugen and Maurice de Saxe and Frederick the Great, deserve to be included in the list of great commanders. Yet even as they fought their various campaigns military thought continued to draw on "the ancients." Taking their works as the acme of wisdom, it contributed little that was fundamentally new.

To cite but one extreme example, when the Marquis de Folard wrote a famous essay on tactics in the 1720s he cast it entirely in the form of a commentary on Polybius and, specifically, the (unsuccessful) combat of Macedonian phalanx against Roman legion. Even to the point where he treated the musket, now fixed with the newly invented bayonet, almost as if it were simply some sort of pike.

After Machiavelli, the first writer whose *oeuvre* must be discussed on these pages is Raimondo Montecuccoli. Montecuccoli was an Italian nobleman who served the Habsburgs continuously from early in the Thirty Years War to his death in 1680. During his career he somehow found time to take an interest in every aspect of the intellectual life of his times including, not least, the occult. His most important work was the *Treatise on War* which was written in 1639–1643 when the author was a prisoner of the Swedes. However, apparently it was seen as a state secret and, though allowed to circulate in manuscript form, was published only long after his death. Foreshadowing the Enlightenment, Montecuccoli's objective was to investigate every part of the art of war at the hand of observation and experience. Next he proposed to draw up detailed rules, and join them into a system which would be subject to reason.

Accordingly, part I discusses preparations for war, including political preparations—the creation of alliances—on the one hand and the amassing of supplies, arms and money on the other. Part II deals with training, discipline, logistics, and intelligence. Montecuccoli, unlike Machiavelli, was a firm advocate of standing, professional forces of the kind which had been pioneered by the Dutch general, Maurice of Nassau. This part also has much to say about the conduct of war, including fortification, marches, operational maneuver—a field in which Montecuccoli was considered a master—and the peculiar tactical difficulties that resulted from the need to combine cavalry with artillery and infantry as well as muskets with pikes. Finally, Part III deals with what we today would call "war termination" and the attainment of a more favorable peace.

A point worth making here, which distinguishes Montecuccoli from previous writers, is that he looks at war as something waged by states rather than by peoples (as in classical Greek and Republican Rome) or rulers (as in China, Imperial Rome, Byzantium, the Middle Ages, and the Renaissance). Explicitly following the ideas of the late sixteenth century political scientist, Justus Lipsius, he clearly distinguishes between external and internal war. Indeed, the point was soon to come where the latter no longer counted as war at all but was downgraded to civil war, revolution, internal dissent, and, in our own day, terrorism. To use a term I previously coined, the age of trinitarian warfare—government against government, regular army against regular army, with the people reduced to a passive role—had dawned.

A century or so after Montecuccoli wrote, Frederick the Great said that Lipsius was hopelessly antiquated and should be thrown out of the window. That was because the Flemish philosopher's ideas of the state as the only legitimate war-making organization were now being taken very much for granted.

On the other hand, and much like his predecessors, Montecuccoli still failed to distinguish between strategy, the operational level, and tactics. As has been well said, war during most of its history consisted mainly of an extended walking tour combined with large scale robbery. Deficient communications prevented the coordination of forces unless they were kept closely together; whereas the short range of weapons meant that active hostilities against the enemy could only get under way on those comparatively rare occasions when armies drew up opposite each other so as to give battle. Though statesmen such as Pericles, and commanders in chief such as Hannibal, clearly had in mind some master plans by which they sought to achieve victory, he who looks for the above mentioned distinctions in any of the writings discussed so far will do so in vain.

Towards the end of Montecuccoli's life the term tactics, derived from the Greek and meaning the ordering of formations on the battlefield, was just beginning to come into use. However, another century had to pass before it was clearly distinguished from strategy in the sense of the conduct of war at the higher level.

To a man, Montecuccoli's eighteenth-century successors continued to write as if tactics, operational art, and strategy were one. To a man, too, they accepted the idea that war was something to be conducted against foreigners in a different, normally but not invariably neighboring, country. Finally, to a man they shared his notion that the purpose of theory was to reduce warfare to a "system" of rules. The latter would be grounded in experience and supported by reason. Obviously this was something that was much easier to do in regard to fields where the enemy's independent will did not have to be taken into consideration. Thus discipline, marches, logistics, and cantonments were easier to encompass than were tactics; tactics, easier than operational art; and operational art, easier than strategy. Hence, as Clausewitz later noted, from about 1690 on there was a tendency for theory to grow from the bottom up, so to speak. It started with the most technical operations. Only then, expanding its horizons, it moved towards greater things.

Montecuccoli having pointed out the things military theory ought to aim at, the first part of the art of war to be reduced to a "system" was, as might be expected, siege warfare. Since the end of the fifteenth century and the beginning of the sixteenth, a period which saw the introduction of the first effective siege artillery on one hand and of the bastion on the other, both the art of attacking and that of defending them had made great strides. By the late seventeenth century the acknowledged master in both fields was a Frenchman, Sebastien le Prestre de Vauban. Vauban, who was of bourgeois origins, was a military engineer. He spent his life alternately building fortifications for Louis XIV or conducting sieges in that king's name. Late in his career he put down his experiences in two slim volumes which dealt with the defense and the attack, respectively. They neither were nor claimed to be a comprehensive treatise on the art of war. On the other hand, and thanks largely to the fact that of all types of military operations siege warfare was the easiest to reduce to rules, they were a model of their kind which others sought to emulate.

The precise ways in which Vauban recommended that fortresses be attacked or defended do not concern us here. Suffice it to say that, in both respects, he proposed an extremely methodical *modus operandi* designed to achieve the objective step by step and with as few casualties as possible. After all, the king's professional soldiers were expensive to raise, equip, and maintain.

Focusing on the attack, the first step was to concentrate an army as well as sufficient supplies of everything needed, including, the men, their arms, ammunition, powder (for mines as well as firearms), engineering materials, and tools. Then it was necessary to isolate the soon to be taken fortress by cutting if off from the outside world, using lines of vallation and counter-vallation for the purpose.

Next a thorough reconnaissance made by the commander in person was to reveal the fortress' weak points. The guns were to be brought up, properly situated, and dug in. The bombardment itself was to be carried out in three bounds as each bound brought the attackers closer to the walls. Sallies by the defenders were to be carefully guarded against and, if they took place nevertheless, allowed to run their course and repulsed before siege operations properly speaking resumed. Breaches were to be systematically widened until they were "practicable." And so on, measure for measure, until the capture—or, even better, the surrender—of the fortress—was obtained.

As of late, attempts have been made to belittle Vauban's originality and deny his historical importance both as a builder and as a commander. Be this as it may, the fact remains that his writings have never been surpassed in their own field. As late as 1830 they were still being reprinted as a practical guide. Meanwhile whatever theoretical wisdom was contributed by others who were active in the field had been long forgotten. One and all, the aim of his successors was to extend his approach to warfare in its entirety, a task in which they invariably failed.

To pass over them rapidly, Jacques Francois de Chastenet, Marquis de Puységur (1655–1743) spent most of his life fighting for Louis XIV in whose army he finally rose to the position of quartermaster general. Written in the 1720s, his *Art of War by Principles and Rules* was explicitly modeled on Vauban. What the latter had done for siege warfare Puységur sought to do for "the entire theory of war from the smallest part to the largest." Seeking to contradict those who claimed that only practice mattered, moreover, he wanted to show that war could be taught "without war, without troops, without an army, without having to leave one's home, simply by means of study, with a little geometry and geography."

Having provided a survey of ancient and modern military writers as well as his own military experience, Puységur explains that "the foundation of the art of war is knowing how to form good *ordres de battaile* and how to make them move and operate according to the most perfect rules of movement, the principles of which are derived from geometry, with which all officers must be familiar." Applying his own recipe step by step, he then illustrates the use of geometrical principles in order to find "the best method" for (*inter alia*) conducting marches, carrying out maneuvers in the face of the enemy, constructing camps, confronting an enemy who may have taken shelter behind lines, rivers, marshes, inundations, woods, and other obstacles, as well as foraging and passing convoys. Having done all this, he concludes with "the movements of two armies advancing upon each other," only to break off his near-endless catalogue of "principles and rules" at precisely at the point where war, understood as an *interaction* of the two sides, begins.

More famous than Puységur was Maurice, also known as the Marshal, de Saxe. A natural son of the Elector of Saxony, he became a professional soldier. Ultimately he was appointed commander in chief of the

French Army during the War of the Austrian Succession (1740–1748). His *Reveries* (Dreams) were written in 1732, allegedly during thirteen feverish nights and with no other aim in mind except that of amusing himself.

On one level the book is a reaction against Puységur. It starts by lamenting the absence of any reference to the "sublime" (i.e. non-mechanical) aspects of war in his predecessor's work. On another it epitomizes eighteenth century warfare at its complex best, assuming as it does two comparatively small armies (at one point, following Montecuccoli, he says that 50,000 is the maximum that can be handled by any general) maneuvering against each other with the aim of fulfilling the sovereign's orders to capture this province or that.

This maneuvering was seen as the essence of war. Battle was to be engaged in only as a last resort; and then only when the prospects for victory appeared certain. There are separate chapters about field warfare, mountain warfare, siege warfare, and the problems of building field fortifications and dealing with them. Unlike many of his contemporaries, moreover, Saxe as a foreign nobleman without an independent fortune had worked his way up the chain of command almost from the bottom. Hence he also had many shrewd observations concerning the need to keep the soldiers' clothing simple and the commander's mind free of excessive detail. And he warned of the danger of making generals out of colonels and thereby risking the possibility that they would be promoted one level above their natural ability.

Generally, though, his most important contribution is considered to be the "legion." Against the background of a period which still did not possess integrated formations comprising all arms—the largest unit was the regiment—he proposed the establishment of such formations. Each one was to number exactly 3,582 men. Each was to comprise, besides four infantry regiments, four troops of horse (one for each regiment), two twelve-pounder guns, a permanent headquarters, transport, engineers, and various supporting services. With that, the need to draw up a detailed *ordre de battaile*, which Puységur had regarded as the very essence of the military art, for each occasion would be obviated. One would simply be able to name a "legion" and send it on this mission or that.

Permanent formations would prove more cohesive than the rest and would be thus able to serve as "a kind of universal seminary of soldiers where different nations are freely adopted and their natural prejudices effectually removed." In any event, the idea of building large, permanent, combined formations was destined to be adopted during the second half of the century and proved critical to the development of the art of war and of strategy in particular. Still, no more than his contemporaries did de Saxe himself distinguish between strategy and tactics.

To round off this chapter, the military works of Frederick the Great must be briefly discussed. Reflecting the typical Enlightenment belief in education, they were produced over a period of some thirty years. First came the *Principes Genereaux* of 1746; this was followed by the *Testament Politique* (1761), the *Testament Militaire* (1768) and the *Éléménts de Castrametrique et de Tactique* (1771) as well as a long didactic poem known as *The Art of War*. Much of this material was originally secret and intended strictly for the use of senior Prussian officers and officials. Accordingly it does not so much deal with the art of war *per se* as to the way in which it ought to be practiced by Prussia, and again the reason for including it here is mainly the fact that its author was undoubtedly one of the greatest commanders of all times.

Prussia, then, is described as an artificial country, spread over much of Germany and Poland, and held together as a work of art. At the center of the work was the army. It alone could guarantee the state's continued existence, and therefore had to be fostered by all means. For both military and political reasons the army's commander was to be the king alone. Not for Frederick the *conseils de guerre* which were common elsewhere and for which he not seldom expressed his contempt, commenting e.g. that France under Louis XV was governed by a cabal of four plus Madame de Pompadour. The officers were to be drawn exclusively from the nobility. That was because the one factor that could make men march into the cannon which are trained at them is honor, and honor was to be found among nobles alone. Frederick was not incapable of putting on a show of gruff appreciation for the rank and file. Still, he firmly believed that the one means to keep them in line was ferocious discipline. As he once said, "they need to fear their officers more than the enemy."

Held together by iron bonds, such an army would be able to march more swiftly, maneuver more precisely, and fire more rapidly than the enemy. Above all, it would be able to take casualties, recover from defeat and fight again. A most important factor, considering the number of battles Frederick lost. With these rock-solid elements in place, he could instruct his generals about the details. Thus, during marches, the army's two wings were not to be separated by more than a few miles. Provisions were to be obtained by "eating everything there is to eat [in a province] and then moving somewhere else." Mountains, swamps, forests and other places capable of offering shelter to deserters were to be avoided as far as possible, and foraging soldiers were to be carefully guarded. The best method of espionage "which always succeeds" was to choose a peasant, arrest his wife as a hostage, and attach to him a soldier disguised as a servant. Next he would be sent into the enemy's camp—an idea which could equally well have come out of some Chinese, or Byzantine, manual. There was something about the use of artillery and cavalry and something about the capture of defended places. Much of what Frederick has to say is incisive and succinct. Limited as it is to his own time and place, however, little of it deserves to be studied by way of a theoretical introduction to war.

By the end of the nineteenth century the king had come to be celebrated as the founder of the Prussian-German Army. To gain respect, any
military action had to be traceable to him. Much ink was spilt over the
question as to whether he preferred annihilation (*Niederwerfung*) over attrition (*Ermattung*) or the other way around. In fact his written works do
not have very much to say about the matter. His views must be deduced
from his practice. On two occasions, then, Frederick engaged in what
today would be called a *Blitzkrieg*. In 1740 he sought to overrun Silesia,
and in 1756 Saxony, before the enemy, who in both cases was Austria,
could react. In both cases the attempt failed. Instead he became involved
in a protracted war which even assumed pan-European dimensions. If
only because two are needed for a fight, broadly speaking in these wars
Frederick showed himself neither more nor less inclined toward fighting
decisive battles than his contemporaries. Such bloodbaths were indeed
frequent. But so, particularly during the latter phases of the Seven Years
War, were lengthy pauses and complicated maneuvers intended to pre-
serve his own forces and outfox the enemy.

As has already been mentioned, several Enlightenment military writers lamented the fact that, unlike the remaining sciences, the one of war
did not have any clear and universally applicable rules. One and all, their
objective in writing was to provide such rules, either for themselves, for
their comrades, for their subordinates, or for a wider readership. Precisely because its scope was limited—it completely ignores both the military and the political context of the fortifications and sieges with which
it deals—among all these works that of Vauban is by far the most successful. Lacking any similar focus, the rest sought to construct "systems"
which would not comprise mere handbooks, but would cover war as a
whole.

Seldom did that attempt succeed. While many authors had interesting things to say, with the possible exception of Saxe and his legions they

are concerned with the technicalities of their own age rather than any-thing that foreshadows the future. Perhaps the best that can be said for them is that, as the growing number of publications in the field proves, they both reflected and were responsible for a situation in which warfare was coming to be considered a fit subject for serious theoretical study. The age of the self-taught officer who was also an entrepreneur was draw-ing to an end. His place was taken by officers who received their commis-sions after having passed through a military academy and later undertook further study at one of the new staff colleges. The latter began to open their doors in Prussia and France from about 1770. In the future it was to the students and graduates of these institutions, above all, that writers on military theory were to address themselves.

4. FROM GUIBERT TO CLAUSEWITZ

IN the military field, as in others, the years leading up to the French Revolution were marked by intellectual ferment. The political system of absolute states, created at Westphalia in 1648, was visibly coming apart at the seams. Both Louis XV and Frederick II were aware that radical change was on the way. The former in particular expressed his hope that the deluge would only come "*après moi.*" The nature of the change was foreshadowed in the work of political writers of whom the most radical one was Rousseau. In the military field, the writer who made the greatest name for himself was a young man named Jacques Antoine Hypolite, Comte de Guibert.

The background to Guibert's work, like that of his late eighteenth century contemporaries, was formed by the Seven Years War. It stood to the period 1763–1789 much as World War I did to the period 1919–1939, as a paradigm. In the Seven Years War, the French Army had performed poorly. It failed to achieve much against Frederick the Great's Prussia even though, together with its allies Austria and Russia, France had enjoyed every economic, numerical, and geographical advantage. Guibert *père* had participated in the Seven Years War as an assistant to the last French commander in Germany, the Marshal de Broglie. The question which occupied Guibert *fils*, who ended that conflict as a colonel, was how to do better next time. Typical of the times in which he lived, he sought to answer the question not merely by offering specific recommendations but by producing a grand "system" of war which would cover the entire subject, both historically and philosophically. The *Essai General de Tactique*, published in 1770 when Guibert was only twenty seven years old, was supposed to represent that system and, at the same time, confer immortality upon its author.

Guibert's detailed recommendations concerning the shape of military formations—he helped write the ordinance of 1791 with which the French Army fought the Revolutionary and Napoleonic Wars, for example—need not concern us here. Four propositions, however, are outstanding and justify the high reputation he enjoyed among his contemporaries. First, to overcome the feebleness so characteristic of France's conduct of the recent conflict, future war should be waged not merely with the aid of the standing army but on the basis of the united forces of the entire nation. Second, to make such participation possible, general conscription was to be introduced. Third, to enable the huge armies that would result to exist without ruining the treasury, the existing logistic system was to be scrapped and war made to feed war. Fourth, those same huge armies were to move not in a single block, as had been standard practice from times immemorial to that of Frederick the Great, but in independent formations of all arms. The last-named demand clearly echoed de Saxe. But it could also rely on the French commander de Broglie. During the later years of the Seven Years War, he became the first to conduct practical experiments with the type of unit later to be known as the division.

However, what really made Guibert famous was not so much the technical details he expounded as his implicit demand for far-reaching political reform which in turn would make possible an army of a completely new kind. Backed by the mobilized nation, such an army thanks to its numbers on the one hand and its patriotic vigor on the other would sweep away its opponents "like reeds before the north wind."

As will be evident from the title of his work, Guibert still did not distinguish between tactics and strategy. At the same time, his distinction between "elementary tactics" (the use of the various arms) and "great tactics" (marching, combat, deployment and encamping) shows that he was groping his way towards the latter concept. Against this background, the term "strategy" was initiated during those very years by another French soldier-scholar, Joly de Maizeroy. Maizeroy too sought to put right the defects which had become apparent in the French Army during the Seven Years War. To do so, he too produced his own "system." As he defined the subject, tactics were "merely mechanical." They included the "composing and ordering of troops [as well as] the manner of marching, maneuvering and fighting" as expounded by Puységur, de Saxe, and others. On the other hand, strategy was concerned with the overall conduct of military operations against the enemy, a field which hitherto had been left almost entirely to the general's intuition.

To call the conduct of war at the higher level by a new name was one thing. To devise principles for it was an entirely different matter, and one whose difficulty had defeated all previous writers if they had even attempted to accomplish it in the first place. The credit of putting together the earliest treatise on strategy belongs to a Prussian officer and writer, Adam Heinrich Dietrich von Bülow. His *Spirit of the Modern System of War* (*Geist des neuern Kriegssystems*) was published in 1799.

An eccentric, arrogant genius who had a knack for alienating people and creating enemies, von Bülow's point of departure was the much improved maps which were becoming available. For example, Roman commanders had maps (judging by the only specimen to have come down to us, the so-called *tabula peutingeriana*) in which only east and west, but not north and south, were indicated. Spanish commanders marching their forces from northern Italy to the Netherlands in the latter half of the sixteenth century had relied on mere sketches to show them the way. Even Vauban, as great an expert on military geography as has ever lived, at various times produced estimates of the surface of France which differed from each other by as much as thirty percent. However, by the time von Bülow wrote the first map of a large country (France) to be based on triangulation rather than on guesswork had just been completed and submitted to the *depot de guerre* in Paris. Several other works aiming to cover other countries in a similar way were approaching completion.

Strategy, then, was the art of conducting war not by means of *coup d'oiel* from behind a horse's ears but in an office, on the surface of a map. Thus regarded, any army once deployed on the border would occupy a base, conceived by von Bülow not as a point but as a definite area with definite dimensions. Depending on geography and the general's intent, a base could be either narrow or wide. Starting from it, the army was to advance upon its objective or objectives; between base and objective there stretched a line, or lines, of operations. Along these lines there flowed supplies and reinforcements in one direction and the wounded, the sick, and prisoners in the other. As of recent times, the growing role played by firearms had greatly increased the demand for ammunition and, in this way, the importance of the lines. It was in them that the key to strategy was to be found.

For example, a general who contemplated an invasion of a neighboring country might advance in one line, two, or more. Depending on the extent of the base as well as the number and location of the objectives selected, these lines might either diverge, or converge, or run parallel to each other. The columns moving along each one might be made equally strong, or else different numbers of troops might be assigned to each. To obtain certainty in such questions (as in any others) it was necessary to resort to mathematics. That made von Bülow's work resemble nothing so much as a textbook in Euclidean geometry. Definitions are provided and followed by propositions, which are then linked to each other by "proofs."

Various possibilities, such as diverging lines and parallel lines, are carefully eliminated. It having been determined that converging lines are best, the remaining question is how far away the objective ought to be. Like the power of gravity, that of the offensive diminishes the further into enemy territory it advances. If the advancing force is not to be cut off by a flanking attack, a definite relationship should be maintained between the length of the line of operations and the width of the base. Thus two lines, stretching from the flanks of the base, should meet at the objective in such a way that they should form a right angle. Proceed further than this—allow a sharp angle to be created—and you risk being cut off by a side-stroke. Thus the entire art of strategy was reduced to a single, simple, geometrical formula.

Von Bülow was not entirely without forerunners. In particular, the British officer and writer Henry Lloyd deserves to be mentioned. However, in claiming that his system of strategy marked "an entirely new" way of looking at war he had right on his side. For centuries if not millenniums past its students had busied themselves with the best method for raising an army; disciplining it; arming and equipping it; building camps for it, provisioning it; adopting this or that marching order; and, when it came to confronting the enemy, either fighting him or tricking him by means of this stratagem or that. What von Bülow did was to shift the emphasis from what we today would have called the organizational, technical, and tactical aspects towards the larger operations of war. No wonder he was carried away by his own discovery. Thus, in the face of unfolding Napoleonic warfare with its numerous climactic battles, he insisted that the correct understanding and adoption of his system of strategic maneuvers would cause battle to disappear. Given that their growing dependence on magazines and lines of operations prevented armies from proceeding very far from their base, he even expected that war itself would be recognized as futile and come to an end. Not that this was a rare belief in the years before 1789 or, more surprisingly, after 1815, 1918, 1945, and 1989.

Von Bülow and his fellow German strategists (for some reason the term strategy caught on much faster in Germany than anywhere else) have often been ridiculed. Nowhere more so than in Tolstoy's great novel, *War and Peace*. The censure is undeserved. Even if wars did not come to an end, his prediction that the art of strategy would work in favor of large states and lead to political consolidation proved correct. What is more, to this day, even those who never heard of von Bülow use the concepts he pioneered such as base, objective, and lines of operations. And they look at strategy in a manner which was largely his making.

From now on, as far as strategy on land was concerned, it only re-mained to work out the details. Nineteenth-century schools of strategy, the multiplying staff colleges, were soon to engage in endless arguments as to whether a single line of operations or a double one, converging or diverging ones, were preferable; and whether to drive them forward (in other words, attack) was easier than maintaining one's base (in other words, defend). Furthermore, as we shall see, von Bülow was by no means the last to try and arrange things in such a way that strategy, expressed in the form of lines, or arrows, on a map, would the place of battle take.

Von Bülow's direct, and much better known, successor was An-toine Henri Jomini. Jomini was a Swiss citizen who saw service under Napoleon and eventually rose to become chief of staff to Marshal Ney. He began his career as a military theorist by throwing his own early es-says, written before he discovered Lloyd and von Bülow, into the fire. His military career was not a great success; still he developed into the high priest of strategy or, as he himself preferred to call it, *les grandes op-*

erations de guerre. Acknowledged or not, his influence has probably not been surpassed even by the great Clausewitz.

Very much like von Bülow, Jomini understood strategy in terms of armed forces moving against each other in two dimensional space. Much more than von Bülow, whose mind tended to work in eighteenth-century geometrical terms, he was prepared to take into account such complicating factors as roads, rivers, mountains, forests, fortresses, and the like which either facilitated maneuver or obstructed it. As with von Bülow, the problem was to discover a "system" which would guide a commander in conducting those maneuvers.

The most important elements of the system remained as before, i.e. bases, objectives, and lines of operations of which there could be various numbers and which stood in various relationships to each other. To these, however, Jomini added a considerable number of other concepts. Some, such as Theaters of Operations (assuming a country engaged against multiple enemies, each of its armies would operate in a separate Theater) and Zones of Operations (the district between an army's base and its objective, through which its communications passed), were to prove useful and made their way into subsequent strategic thought. Others merely injected unnecessary complexity and, some would say, incomprehensibility.

All armies, then, necessarily had lines of operation or, as we would say today, communications. Earlier commanders such as Alexander, Julius Caesar, or even Gustavus Adolphus during the first half of the seventeenth century, had been able to survive and operate for years in enemy territory while maintaining only the most tenuous ties with home. Now, however, the whole point of the art of war was to cut one's enemy's lines of operations without exposing one's own. Doing so would lead to the enemy's surrender, as actually happened to the Austrians at Ulm in 1805, or else to a battle in which he would be placed at a grave disadvantage, as happened to the Austrians at Marengo in 1800 and to the Prussians at

Jena in 1806. Thus was born the *manoeuvre sur les derrieres*, a method of operation by which one part of the army would hold the enemy while the other, if possible while using some natural obstacle in order to conceal and protect itself, would march around him and fall upon his rear.

As Jomini very sensibly wrote, an army with two different lines of operations running back to two different bases would be less exposed to this sort of maneuver than its enemy who possessed only one. Particularly if the lines in question formed an obtuse angle rather an acute one. The fact that he spoke of the theater of war as a "chessboard" and presented his idea in an old-fashioned geometric manner reminiscent of von Bülow detracts nothing from its validity.

The second most important maneuver advocated by Jomini consisted of operating on internal (what von Bülow called diverging) lines. A blue army might find itself between two red ones. That was what had happened to Napoleon during his Italian campaign of 1796 and again in those of 1813 and 1814. Such a situation was not without its dangers. But it was also a source of opportunity. Separated from each other, the red forces would find it difficult to unite and thus bring superior force to bear. Conversely, the blue army was already concentrated and only a short distance away from each red force. These advantages might be used to deliver a swift, sharp blow at one red force before the other could intervene. Next, blue would turn around and the process would be repeated against the other. A perfect example, and one which shows the continuing relevance of Jomini even in the age of air warfare which he never contemplated, is Israel's conduct of the 1967 war against three Arab countries. Each of whom, being separated from the rest by long and tenuous lines of communications, was attacked and defeated in its turn.

Whatever the precise maneuver selected, it was always a question of bringing superior force to bear against the decisive point. Given their importance as centers of communication, capitals were always decisive points. So, to a lesser degree, were road junctions, river crossings, fortresses which blocked or dominated a road, and the like. Another type of decisive point was one from which red's line of operations could be threatened, forcing him either to retreat from his positions or else turn around and fight. If he tried to do the second without doing the first his forces would become divided. That in turn might present blue with an opportunity to beat them in detail.

In a certain sense, the maneuvers advocated by Jomini had always existed. From at least Hannibal on, armies had not only fought each other front to front but sought to outflank each other and surround each other. Before the middle of the 18th century, however, by and large there were no lines of operations to threaten or cut. Moreover, as explained earlier, primitive communications and the fact that no formations of all arms existed compelled armies to stick closely together and only permitted them to engage each other in battle by mutual consent. Given the vastly increased forces made available by the introduction of general conscription in 1791, first Carnot and then Napoleon had been compelled to disperse them and form them into formations of all arms whether they wanted to or not. Once the machinery for commanding such dispersed formations had also been created in the form of the *état major*, these changes greatly increased the repertoire of strategic maneuvers. It was the later that Jomini put into systematic form and codified.

Jomini's earliest work on strategy, the *Treatise on Grand Operations of War*, was published in 1805. It was submitted to Napoleon who, according to its author, expressed his appreciation. From that point on he steadily added to it without, however, changing its essence. In his most mature work, *The Art of War* (1837) he had much to say about the political uses to which war could be put and also about the resources and military institutions of different states. At the same time he extended his theory to include formations, tactics, various kinds of special operations such as the crossing of rivers, and logistics. The last-named were defined as "the practical art of moving armies." There is even a short chapter on "Descents, or Maritime Expeditions." If Clausewitz in *vom Kriege* accused Jomini of having concentrated merely on strategy to the detriment of the political side of war, this is due to the fact that the Prussian general did not live to see his rival's most mature work.

More to the point, Jomini like all his Enlightenment predecessors sought to create a "system" which would tell a commander how to conduct war on the higher level. Particularly in his earlier works, this objective forced him to present war as more rational than it really is, given that only the rational can be systematically analyzed, systematized, and taught. The same was even more true of the Enlightenment as a whole. From about 1770 on, this view came under attack at the hand of the nascent Romantic Movement which insisted that the emotions of the heart, not calculations of the merely mechanical brain, stood at the center of human life. In the military field the most important critic was yet another Prussian officer, diplomat and scholar, Georg Heinrich von Berenhorst.

Published in three volumes between 1796 and 1799, Berenhorst's *Reflections on the Art of War* began with a survey of military history. Antiquity had been the great period when the art of war, emerging from its primitive stage where it had been confined to raids, ambushes, skirmishes and the like, was perfected. Then came a long medieval interval marked by nothing but ignorance and disorder; then at some point between Machiavelli and Montecuccoli (Berenhorst had in mind Maurice of Nassau, the early seventeenth-century Dutch commander) order was restored and progress resumed. The very nature of their quest, however, had led all subsequent authors to overestimate the role of immutable laws while underestimating that of the unknown, uncontrollable forces of human will and emotion.

Soldiers were more than robots who could fire so and so many rounds a minute. An army was not simply a machine moving along this axis or that and carrying out evolutions as its commander directed. It was the ever-variable, often unpredictable, state of mind of commanders and troops, and not simply calculations pertaining to time, distance, and the angles between lines of operations which governed victory and defeat, to say nothing about the role played by that great incalculable, chance.

These arguments were illustrated by referring to Frederick the Great. To the majority of late eighteenth-century commentators the king was perhaps *the* greatest commander of recent times. His maneuvers, particularly the famous "oblique approach" in which one wing attacked the enemy while the other was kept back, were assiduously studied. Berenhorst, however, pointed to the fact that during some ten years of active operations in three wars (the First, Second, and Third Silesian Wars) those maneuvers had been carried out no more than two or three times. Those few and far-apart occasions aside, Frederick was primarily a drillmaster. Time after time he forced his troops into murderous battles. Those battles were won—if they were won, for Frederick's defeats were about as numerous as his victories—only by virtue of iron discipline and sheer force of will.

Well written and provided with plentiful examples, Berenhorst's work was extremely popular during the years immediately after 1800. He and Jomini formed opposite poles. The one emphasized the rational conduct of war at the hand of the strategist, the other, its essential irrationality, unpredictability, and dependence on chance. Both strands of thought were to be united in the greatest of all Western writers on war, Carl von Clausewitz. Given that he too was a child of his times and went through the same tumultuous events as everyone else, to say exactly what qualified him to play this role is not easy. In the production of military theory, as so many other aspects of life, room ought to be left for genius.

Clausewitz's own life has been told so many times that we can all
but skip it here. The essential point is that, while in his mid-twenties,
this unusually earnest and well-read officer began to take a serious interest in military theory. There followed his participation in the disastrous
campaign of 1806, a period spent as a prisoner of war in France, and an
appointment to the General Staff in Berlin. There he helped Scharnhorst,
his revered master, rebuild the Prussian Army. By 1811 his talents as a
theoretician were already sufficiently well known for him to be entrusted
with teaching the Crown Prince (the subsequent Friedrich Wilhelm IV)
about war. In 1812 he found himself with the Russian Army that was
fighting Napoleon in Russia. During the campaigns of 1813–1815 he
was active as a staff officer and in 1817 assumed administrative control
of the Berlin Staff College or Kriegsakademie. Rising to the rank of general, it was there that he produced his great work. The palace in which the
Akademie was located was destroyed by bombing in World War II. Later
it was rebuilt, but no one who works there now can point to Clausewitz's
study or is even familiar with his name.

Like almost all other military writers since 1800, Clausewitz wanted
to penetrate the secret of Revolutionary and Napoleonic warfare which, as
he and the rest saw, clearly differed from what had gone before. Some had
sought that secret in the mobilization of all national resources advocated
by Guibert and made possible by the Revolution. Others, in the conduct
of strategy as explained by von Bülow and, above all, Jomini. Clausewitz,
however was not simply a thoughtful soldier but a true philosopher in
uniform. While accepting that the Revolution had made it possible for
war to be waged "with the full energy of the nation," he sought to go back
to first principles.

This he did by focusing on two questions, to wit: 1. What war was;
and 2. What purpose it served. From the answers to these, and while
constantly checking his thought against both military history and actual

experience, he sought to deduce all the rest. His approach was therefore both deductive and inductive. He discusses the ways in which war ought to be studied as well as the purpose which such study ought to serve. His purpose was not to go into the details of armament and formations, let alone to offer a solution for every problem that might arise. According to Clausewitz, the purpose of studying war was to provide commanders with a sound basis for their thinking and render it unnecessary to reinvent the wheel with every new situation. In the eyes of some informed readers, the pages which deal with this aspect of the problem are the best and most enduring part of his entire *opus*.

To answer the first question Clausewitz in the last book of *On War* constructed an imaginary picture of "absolute war." Meaning, war as it would have been if, stripped of all practical considerations concerning time, place, and intent, it had been able to stand up naked, so to speak. This device, borrowed from the contemporary philosopher Immanuel Kant, enabled him to define war as an elemental act of violence in which all ordinary social restrains were cast off. Since force would naturally invite the use of greater force, war also possessed an inherent tendency towards escalation. That made it essentially uncontrollable and unpredictable, "a great passionate drama." As such it was not primarily a question of acting in accordance with specific principles or rules. Instead it represented the domain of danger, friction, and uncertainty. Its successful conduct was above all a question of possessing the qualities needed in order to counter and master these inherent characteristics. Where those qualities were to come from is another question, into which he refuses to enter.

Clausewitz also had much to say about willpower, bravery, and endurance both in the commander—whose "genius" they formed—and in the army which, from top to bottom, had to be imbued with "military virtue." Though allowing the use of every expedient and requiring the full participation of the intellect, at its core, war was not a question of knowledge, but of character.

Much like his immediate predecessors, Clausewitz distinguished between tactics, which he called the art of winning battles, and strategy, which he defined as the art of using battles to gain the objectives of the campaign. More fundamentally, though, war was a duel between two independent minds. Its interactive nature sharply differentiated it from other activities. To paraphrase, making swords (which only involved acting upon dead matter) was one thing. Using them against another swordsman who is capable of parrying one's own thrusts and replying with others of his own is quite another.

In a brief but brilliant discussion of the theory of war, Clausewitz acknowledges that the system proffered by each of his predecessors contained some elements of truth. Yet no system ought to be allowed to obscure the elemental fact that war consisted of fighting and that fighting—in other words, battle—determined the outcome of wars. No amount of fancy maneuvering could do any good unless it was backed up with a big, sharp sword.

Furthermore, and given the high degree of uncertainty and friction involved, Clausewitz tended to belittle the effect of maneuver, surprise, and stratagems of every kind. Trying to achieve victory by such means was well and good. However, the higher the level at which war was waged, and the greater the masses which took part in it, the less likely they were to achieve decisive results. "The best strategy is always to be very strong, first in general and then at the decisive point." War was "a physical and moral struggle by means of the former." Since the enemy's strength was concentrated in his armed forces, the first objective of strategy ought always to be to smash them. This achieved, his capital could be captured and his country occupied. Thus, compared to much of what had gone before from the time of Montecuccoli on (and to much of what was to come later during the second half of the twentieth century), Clausewitz's *On War* puts forward a brutally realistic doctrine. Clausewitz himself says as much.

Still continuing with strategy, and to illustrate the way in which Clausewitz proceeds from first principles, consider his discussion of the relationship between attack and defense that had occupied many previous authors. The outstanding quality of the attack, he writes, is the delivery of a blow. The outstanding quality of the defense is the need to wait for that blow and parry it. Since anything that does not happen favors the defense, it is easier to defend than to attack, all else being equal. Moreover, the farther away an attacker gets from his base the greater his logistic difficulties and the more forces he will lose owing to the need to leave behind garrisons, safeguard his communications, and the like. Conversely, falling back on his base, the defender will gather his forces and reinforce them. In the end, and it is here that Clausewitz shows his originality over his predecessors, inevitably there will come a "culminating point." The attack will turn into a defense and the defense into an attack. That is, unless the enemy has been smashed and a decisive victory has been won first.

However, Clausewitz provided more than a brief summary of the inherent qualities of war. War was not simply a phenomenon in its own right. As a product of social intercourse it was, or at any rate ought to be, a deliberate political act. "A continuation of policy by other means," to quote the single most celebrated clause he ever wrote. It is true that war had a grammar of its own, i.e. rules which could not be violated with impunity. But it was equally true that it did not have a logic of its own. That logic was to be provided to it from outside, so to speak. Unless its higher conduct and general character were governed by policy, war would be "a senseless thing, without an object."

Translated into practical terms, this view of war as an instrument meant that ultimately its conduct had to be laid down not by the commander in chief but by the political leadership. What is more, it enabled Clausewitz to argue that war was morally neutral—as he says—thus once again allowing his tendency towards brutal realism to come to the fore. "There can be no war without bloodshed; in dangerous things such as war, errors committed out of a feeling of benevolence are the worst." Consequently, in the entire massive work, the only sentence devoted to the law of war is one in which he says that it is so weak and unimportant as to be virtually negligible.

Towards the end of his life Clausewitz, possibly because the Napoleonic Wars were slowly falling into perspective, underwent a change of mind. He now began to recognize that, besides aiming at the "total overthrow" of the enemy, as would follow from his theoretical premises, another kind of war might be possible whose objectives were more limited. He had started to revise his work when he died, leaving behind a mass of unfinished drafts. Whether, had he lived, he would have been able to maintain his original framework or been forced to replace it with another is impossible to say. The question was, how to reconcile war's essentially unlimited nature with its use as a tool in the hand of policy. When he died, he had still not found an answer.

Among Western writers on war, the position of Clausewitz is unique. To resort to a metaphor, his is not an ordinary cookbook full of recipes concerning the utensils and ingredients which, correctly used, will yield certain foods. Instead it contents itself with explaining the nature of cooking and the uses to which it is put, leaving the reader to proceed on his own. As a result, when technological progress caused organization, tactics, and much of strategy to change he alone retained his relevance. Admittedly some of the details of *On War* are without enduring interest. For instance, the discussion of the relationship between the three arms and the methods for attacking a convoy are of little relevance today. But the book as a whole holds up remarkably well as "a treasure of the human spirit."

Thus to compare Clausewitz's advice on this or that detail with that which is proffered by his Western predecessors and contemporaries is to do him an injustice. Unlike them he was a philosopher of war. Only the Chinese classics rival him in this respect, albeit that *their* underlying philosophy is radically different. Clausewitz's way of thought goes back to Aristotle and is based on the distinction between means and ends. By contrast, it is a fundamental characteristic of *Chinese* thought that such a distinction is absent—to Lao Tzu and his followers, admitting its existence would constitute a departure from *dao*. Accordingly, the Chinese texts regard war not as an instrument for the attainment of this end or that but as the product of stern necessity, something which must be confronted and coped with and managed and brought to an end. Clausewitz emphasizes that war is brutal and bloody and seeks to achieve a great victory. By contrast, the Chinese texts are permeated by a humanitarian approach and have as their aim the restoration of *dao*.

These underlying philosophical differences cause Clausewitz to recommend the use of maximum force, the Chinese of minimum force. In turn, the Chinese emphasis on minimum force leads to a greater emphasis on trickery of every sort than Clausewitz, with his realistic assessment of such factors as uncertainty and friction, regards as practicable. Had the two sides met, then Sun Tzu and Co. would undoubtedly have accused Clausewitz of overemphasizing brute strength, which in turn means encouraging stupidity and barbarism. Clausewitz on his part would have replied that the kind of super-sophisticated warfare advocated by them was intellectually attractive but, alas, often unrealistic and sometimes dangerous as excessive maneuvering provided the enemy with opportunities to "cut off one's head." None of this is to deny that, in practice, Western warfare often made use of stratagems whereas Chinese warfare could be quite as bloody and brutal as its Western counterpart. Indeed it could be more so, given that necessity has no limits and that questions regarding the law of war *a la* Bonet would have made the sages put on a contemptuous smile.

These considerations explain why Clausewitz and the Chinese were able to transcend their own time and place. Still, inevitably, their reputations had their ups and downs. Outside China itself, where Sun Tzu and Confucius served as the basis for the state-run examination system, the Chinese writings were particularly popular during the eighteenth-century craze for *chinoiserie* as well as after the Chinese Revolution in 1949. There are currently at least *five* different English translations of Sun Tzu on the market. As for Clausewitz, after being greatly venerated during the nineteenth century he was often regarded as "too philosophical" during the first half of the twentieth. His nadir probably came during the early years of the nuclear era when he was relegated to the sidelines, only to make an impressive comeback after 1973, when a new English translation appeared and the Arab-Israeli war encouraged people to think about large scale conventional warfare.

More ups and downs are to be expected. One recent historian even speaks of the "Grand Old Tradition of Clausewitz-Bashing." Yet is it likely that, when all the rest are forgotten, Sun Tzu and Clausewitz will still be read and studied by those who seek to achieve a serious theoretical understanding of war. Considering that even the "modern" Clausewitz is now almost two hundred years old, this constitutes high praise indeed.

5. The Nineteenth Century

An aspect of Clausewitz's thought not yet discussed in these pages, and which distinguishes it from virtually all his predecessors, is the way he approached history. As we saw, the Chinese classics were written between 400 and 200 BC. The background was a semi-mythological past regarded as superior to the present. With the exception of Vegetius, who resembles the Chinese in this respect, in the extant treatises written by ancient military theorists a sense of historical change is almost entirely lacking. The same is true of the Byzantine and medieval texts. Severely practical, the former are really little more than handbooks. They are interested solely in the present, and exclude any hint concerning the possibility that the past has been, or the future could be, different. The latter are usually aware of the glorious if idolatrous past. But somehow they manage to combine this awareness with a complete disregard for the immense differences that separated their own times from those of, say, Vegetius.

The position of "modern" Western authors from Machiavelli on is more complicated. Regarding themselves as emerging from centuries of barbarism, the men of the fifteenth century were acutely aware of their own inferiority *vis à vis* the ancient world in every field, the military one included. Accordingly, for them it was a question not so much of seeking innovation as of recovering and assimilating the achievements of that world.

No one was more representative of these attitudes than Machiavelli, to whom the very idea of outdoing his admired Romans would have been sacrilege. But it was equally evident in his successors. Throughout the eighteenth century, most writers on military affairs insisted that the best authors to study were Frontinus and Vegetius and, among historians, Polybius, Caesar, and Livy. Thus Joly de Maizeroy not only translated the Byzantine classics from the Greek but was regarded as the leading expert on ancient warfare, a subject on which he wrote several specialized studies. Both Bülow and Berenhorst begin their works by comparing ancient warfare with that of the modern age.

And yet, even with Bülow, the situation began to change. For von Bülow this was because the ancient textbooks had absolutely nothing to say about strategy, precisely the field to which he himself had made the greatest contribution, of which he was understandably proud. That also accounts for the fact that, as with Jomini, "the ancients" are not even mentioned in Clausewitz's book.

Another, perhaps more important factor, was the overall intellectual climate in which Clausewitz and Jomini wrote. As the Enlightenment gave way to the Romantic Movement, philosophers such as Vico and Hegel began propagating a view of history which emphasized the "otherness" of the past rather than its essential similarity with the present. Until then history had been seen as a record of the same thing happening again and again. That was why centuries-old events could serve as a source for practical lessons. Now history was transformed into the record of change. In general, the more temporally distant the period, the greater the gulf that separated it from what was to follow.

This is not the place to follow the transformation of history, a subject better left to specialized students of that subject. Suffice it to say that, by the time Clausewitz did his main work in the 1820's, it had been fully accomplished. Previously most of the authors here discussed had assumed that, since history was essentially unchanging, war too had unchanging principles. However, to Clausewitz, whose approach was "historicist," this was much less evident. In Book VIII of *vom Kriege* he comes very close to saying that, since each period made war in a manner corresponding to its social and political characteristics, a single theory of war applicable to all times and places might not be possible at all.

Clausewitz saw himself as a practical soldier writing for other practical soldiers (the first edition of his book was sold by subscription). Hence he was in some doubt as to how far back one could go in one's quest for rules, lessons, principles, and examples. Whether, in other words, "modern" history began with the campaigns of Frederick the Great; or with the end of the War of the Spanish Succession; or with the Peace of Westphalia which had marked the construction of the modern European State. Be that as it may, he felt quite certain that, since only recent events were at all like the present, the further back one went the less useful the things one could find. His own writings on military history only go as far back as Gustavus Adolphus. Previous wars, such as those of the Tartars and the middle ages, are mentioned only to emphasize their "otherness." As to the ancient authors, they are entirely ignored. None is even allowed to make his appearance on the pages of *On War.*

Even ignoring the contemporary revolution in historical thought, it was becoming all too clear that the old tried-and-true methods for thinking about war would no longer suffice. Between 217 BC, when Ptolemy IV had confronted Antiochus III at Raffia, and Leipzig in 1813 the maximum number of men who had confronted each other in battle had scarcely grown. It is true that, at some point located approximately three-quarters through the time that separated the first from the second of these battles, firearms in the form of muskets and cannon had largely taken over from edged weapons. Even so, battle remained very much what it had always been. In other words, a question of men standing up, at a certain carefully defined time and space (battles tended to be over in a few hours and seldom took up more than a few square kilometers), in relatively tight formations (throughout the eighteenth century there had been an intense debate on the relative merits of the column versus the line), and fighting each other in full view of each other. Thus Napoleon towards the end of his career was able to boast of having commanded in no fewer than sixty "pitched battles" (*battailes rangèes*). A phrase that speaks for itself.

By the middle of the nineteenth century, these parade-like clashes were becoming obsolete. New, quick-firing weapons started making their appearance from about 1830 on. The outcome was to make the amount of firepower which could be produced per unit and per minute leap upwards as well as leading to dramatic improvements in accuracy and range. These developments made it questionable whether men would still be able to fight while standing on their feet and confronting each other in a relatively tight formation. As one might expect, a period of experimentation followed, nowhere more so than in the United States. There, during the Civil War, commanders who had never previously been in charge of large units and amateurish troops less bound to the past than many of their professional colleagues across the Atlantic did not hesitate to break formation, seek shelter, and adopt camouflage clothing when they thought doing so could save their lives. Confining our view to written military thought, however, one of the first and most important authors who attempted to come to grips with the new phenomenon was a French officer, Charles Jean Jacques Joseph Ardant du Picq.

In one sense, as he says, the work of du Picq represented a reaction against the geometrical approach of von Bülow and Jomini. Conversely, though he does not mention them, he followed Berenhorst and Clausewitz. Like them, he considered that the key to war was to be found not in any clever maneuvers, let alone geometrical formula, but in the heart of man. Much more than Clausewitz in particular, who served explicit warning against indulging in mere idle talk about the last-named subject, he was prepared to try and look into the factors which rendered that heart at least partly immune to the terror of battle. Du Picq saw considerable active service in the Crimea, Syria and Algeria. Hence he was under no illusion that it could be rendered anywhere near *completely* immune.

Trying to find out what made men fight, du Picq resorted to two different methods. One was detailed studies of ancient warfare when battles had been "simple and clear" and sources, in the form of Polybius, impeccable. The other was a questionnaire which he sent out to his fellow officers. This enabled him to interview them very closely about the way their men behaved in combat and the factors which influenced them. In any event, the Franco-Prussian War broke out, and du Picq himself was killed before he received many answers. Not that it mattered, for by that time most of his *Battle Studies* were largely complete and his mind had been made up.

Fighting against non-European peoples, du Picq had witnessed the power of military organization at first hand. Had not Napoleon said that, whereas one Mamluk was the equal of three Frenchmen, a hundred Frenchmen could confidently take on five times their number in Mamluks? Individual men were often cowards; however, having trained together and standing together in formation, they were transformed. A new social force, known as cohesion, made its appearance as comrade sustained comrade and mutual shame prevented each one from running away.

To paraphrase, four men who do not know each other will hesitate to confront a lion. But once they know each other and feel they can trust each other they will do so without fear. *That*, rather than any clever evolutions which it might carry out, was the secret of the ancient Greek and Macedonian phalanx in which men, packed closely together in their ranks and files, sustained each other and, if necessary, physically pushed each other into battle while preventing any escape. The phalanx was, however, if anything too closely packed. As a result, those in front had no way to break away and rest from their ordeal. In the meantime, those in the rear were almost as exposed to the fury of battle as their comrades in front. The chequerboard formation of the Roman legion was much better. Made up of carefully placed smaller units, and arrayed in three successive lines (*acies*), it enjoyed all the advantages of the phalanx. All this, while still enabling the majority of combatants to catch their breath and recuperate between bouts of fighting.

Now to the really decisive question: namely, how to ensure that men did not break in front of the five rounds per minute which could be directed at them by contemporary weapons. Du Picq's answer was that greater reliance should be placed upon skirmishers, and that "every officer should be reduced who does not utilize them to some degree." Skirmishers, however, should be closely controlled. There was no point in sending them so far ahead that, feeling isolated, they would merely hide or run. Controlling the skirmishers was the job of the battalion commander (since the battalion was the largest unit whose commander could still be in direct touch with the rank and file during battle, du Picq tended to disregard the activities of more senior officers). To enable him to do so the size of the battalions should be cut down by one third, from six to four companies. As one battalion engaged in skirmishing another ought to be left standing close by, sustaining its sister in the manner of the Roman maniples. The contemporary view of gaps in the line as dangerous was mistaken; on the contrary, and still in the manner of the Roman maniples, such gaps had to be deliberately used in order to enable some battalions to advance towards the enemy and the remainder to rest. Care should be taken that the supporting troops belong to the same units as the skirmishers, and *vice versa*. Any attempt to make troops fire on command should be discouraged.

During his lifetime the work of du Picq, whose professional career was anything but extraordinary, drew little attention. This, however, changed during the late 1890s. At that time the French Army, having recovered from the defeat of 1870–71, began looking for a method by which it might one day attack and defeat the superior German Army so as to regain Alsace-Lorraine. *Battle Studies* was disinterred, and its author turned into the patron-saint of the *Furor Galicus* School of warfighting. Good organization, unit cohesion, thorough training, firm command, patriotism, and the alleged native qualities of the French soldier were to turn him into an irresistible fighting animal. After all, had not Ammianus Marcelinus in the fourth century AD described that soldier's ancestors as "tall of stature, fair and ruddy, terrible for the fierceness of their eyes, fond of quarreling, and overbearing insolence"? In the autumn of 1914 that approach, complete with the famous *pantalons rouges*, led straight into the muzzles of the waiting German machine guns. But for this du Picq, who had always emphasized the power of the defense and who had spent much of his professional career worrying lest modern soldiers would *not* be able to confront modern fire, can scarcely be blamed.

Partly because he never rose beyond colonel, partly because his main interest was the heart of man and the factors which enabled it to function in battle, du Picq has very little to say about strategy. To the majority of officers, however, strategy was the key to large-scale war. They saw it as an esoteric branch of knowledge they alone possessed and which was intellectually much more satisfying than any mere psychological analysis of the rank and file could ever be. Accordingly, throughout the first half of the nineteenth century the most important military theoretician by far was considered to be Jomini. The rumor that American Civil War-era generals carried him in their pockets may be exaggerated. But there is no doubt that his influence can be discerned e.g. in the Antietam and Chancellorsville campaigns as well as in Sherman's march through Georgia to South Carolina.

What was more, just as the new rapid-firing arms began to transform combat after 1830, strategy was revolutionized by the introduction of railways. Hitherto lines of communications had been somewhat nebulous concepts. Now they were reconstructed in a new, cast-iron form anyone could trace on the ground or on a map. Clearly here was a novel instrument which had to be mastered if it was to be successfully harnessed to war and conquest.

This is not the place to outline the impact of railways on strategy and logistics, a topic that has been the subject of several excellent monographs. Suffice it to say that, outside the US (which, however, produced no military-theoretical writings of any importance) nobody was more closely associated with their use for war and conquest than the Prussian chief of staff, Helmuth von Moltke. Moltke, who was born in 1800, rose to prominence through sheer intellectual qualities rather than by way of practical experience. In fact, he never commanded any unit larger than a battalion. Though he possessed a well-educated pen, he never wrote a single definitive work. His thought must be garnered from the campaigns he conducted so successfully. To this must be added the series of great memoranda which, in his capacity of chief of the general staff, he wrote between about 1857 and 1873. At heart a practitioner rather than theoretician, Moltke did not bother to go into first principles. Nor does he mention any of his predecessors. On the other hand, his memoranda do display a unity and a cohesion which justifies including him in the present study.

To simplify, Moltke's starting point was the rise in the size of armies that had taken place as a result of growing population and industrialization. Instead of tens of thousands, they now numbered hundreds of thousands. Even a single corps, comprising some 30,000 men, was so large that its sub-units would take an entire day to pass a single point. As a result, the trains, making up the rear, would never be able to catch up with the leading elements. Prussia moreover, was the smallest of the five leading European Powers. To compensate, alone among those powers it had retained a form of universal conscription. Having spent two, later three, years under the colors the conscripts were sent home but remained on call in case of an emergency. The problem was how to mobilize them quickly and deploy them on the frontier, and it was here that the railways came in handy.

At the time Moltke was appointed chief of the General Staff it was merely a department inside the War Ministry responsible for training, preparation, and armament. Going to work, he drew up extremely detailed plans for using the railways to carry out mobilization and deployment. Rehearsed in 1859 and in 1864, in 1866 they took the world's breath away as the Prussian Army mobilized with an efficiency, and at a speed, which had previously been considered unattainable. What was more, and as Moltke had expressly foreseen, attaining maximum speed in mobilization meant that as many railways as possible had to be utilized simultaneously. Together with the sheer size of the forces ("a concentrated army is a calamity: it cannot subsist, it cannot move, it can only fight") this meant that the troops would be strung out along much of the frontier. A strategy of interior lines of the kind that had been recommended by Jomini and regarded as perhaps *the* one most important device of all would thereby become impossible.

To Moltke, therefore, strategy remained what it had been from Bülow on. It was, first, a question of moving large forces about in two-dimensional space so as to put them in the most favorable position for combat; and second, making use of the outcome of combat after it had taken place. Like du Picq, however, he realized that the rise of quick-firing weapons had caused the balance between offense and defense to change. To attack frontally in the face of rifles, such as the French Chassepots, which were sighted to 1,200 yards and capable of accurately firing six rounds a minute was suicide. Much better to look for the enemy's flank and envelop him. In this way the deployment in width, which contemporary critics such as Friedrich Engels regarded as madness when it was used against Austria in 1866, was turned into a virtue. The enemy would be caught between armies coming from two, possibly three, directions, and be crushed between them. Moltke, in a letter he wrote to the historian Heinrich von Treitschke in 1873, called this "the highest feat which strategy can achieve." Strategically speaking, Moltke intended his armies to take the offensive. Tactically the troops were supposed to use their firepower and remain on the defense, although in practice that order was not always obeyed.

To carry out the mobilization and coordinate the moves of his widely-dispersed forces Moltke made use of another new technical instrument, the telegraph. If only because the railways themselves could only be operated to maximum effect if the trains' movements were carefully coordinated, wires and tracks tended to run in parallel. This enabled Moltke to implement his strategy of external lines *and* remain in control, previously an unheard-of feat. The contemporary telegraph was, however, a slow instrument. The fact that wiretapping had been practiced both during the American Civil War and in the Austrian-Prussian War required encryption and decryption procedures at both ends, slowing down the lines' capacity. Again turning necessity into a virtue—the mark of a truly great general—Moltke devised his system of directives or *Weisungen*. He insisted that orders be short and only tell subordinate commanders what to do, but not how.

The system presupposed very good acquaintance and strong mutual trust between officers. That in turn meant that it was possible only thanks to that élite institution, the General Staff. The latter had its representatives in every major unit. In time it spread from the top down, until in 1936 the volume known as *Truppenfuehrung* (Commanding Troops) announced that "war demands the free *independent* commitment of every soldier from the private to the general." The result was a uniquely flexible, yet cohesive, war machine that was the envy of the world.

As already mentioned, unlike many of his eighteenth and nineteenth century predecessors Moltke never produced a "system." He did, indeed, go on record as saying that strategy itself was but a "system of expedients." War has a penchant for turning the victor into a fool, however, and post-1871 Imperial Germany was no exception. As Moltke himself noted during his later years—he was to remain in office until 1888, when he could barely any longer mount a horse—the younger generation at the General Staff did not possess their predecessors' broad vision. Instead, possibly because of the attention they paid to the railways, an instrument regarded as the key to victory and requiring painstaking attention to detail, they tended to be technically-inclined and narrow minded. Nobody exemplified these tendencies more than the next writer with whom we must concern ourselves here, Alfred von Schlieffen. Born in 1833, in 1891 he was appointed chief of the General Staff. By that time the latter, far from being an obscure department in the *Kriegsministerium*, had become the most prestigious single institution in Germany with overall responsibility for preparing the land army and leading it into war.

From 1893, the year in which Germany and Russia concluded an alliance, Schlieffen's problem was to prepare his country for war on two fronts. The basic assumption was that Germany was the smaller power caught between two others which, together, were stronger than it was. Hence it could not afford to remain on the defensive, leading to a long and acrimonious debate concerning the respective virtues of annihilation versus attrition. But against which of the two enemies should the Germans concentrate first? Schlieffen decided on France, suggesting that its capacity for rapid mobilization made it into the more dangerous enemy. Moreover, geographical circumstances—compared with Russia, France was small—would permit the delivery of a rapid knock-out blow. Like his late nineteenth century contemporaries, however, Schlieffen was well aware that advancing technology, including, by now, barbed wire, mines, machine guns, and cannon provided with recoil mechanisms, favored the defense. Furthermore, the French border had been fortified. Hence he decided that an outflanking movement was needed; and, after considering a left hook and a right one, finally settled on an advance through Belgium.

Having ruminated on all this for years, and having prepared the great Plan which will be forever associated with his name, on 1 January 1906 Schlieffen stepped down from his post. In the same year he produced his theoretical "masterpiece," a three-page article entitled "Cannae" after the battle fought by Hannibal against the Romans in 216 BC. From this as well as his other essays, especially "The Warlord" and "War in the Modern Age," one may form an idea of the way he, as the general in charge of the most powerful and most sophisticated military machine the world had ever seen, understood war. Tactics and logistics apart (he never showed much interest in either of them) war was the clash of large armies (he never showed any interest in navies) maneuvering against each other in two dimensional space. The objective of this maneuvering was to annihilate (*vernichten*) the other side with the greatest possible dispatch. Anything else, though perhaps admissible under particular circumstances, was considered a lesser achievement.

To annihilate the enemy it was not enough to simply push him back by applying pressure to his front. Given the superior power, under modern conditions, of both the tactical and the strategic defense, such a procedure would merely result in an "ordinary" victory after which the enemy, though forced to retreat, would be able to reorganize and renew the struggle. The trick, therefore, was to hold the enemy in front while taking him in flank, driving him off his lines of communications, and, ideally, forcing him to surrender. That was what Moltke had succeeded in doing at Sedan in 1870. To Schlieffen's credit, it should be said that he did not believe it was simply a question of geometry. An alert enemy would not allow himself to be outflanked easily. Therefore, he had to be *enticed* into making the wrong moves. "For a great victory to be won the two opposing commanders must cooperate, each one in his way (*auf seiner Art*). To a critic who once told him that the art of war was at bottom a simple one, he responded: "Yes, all it turns on is this stupid question of winning."

With Schlieffen, we have arrived at the end of the "long" nineteenth century. It started auspiciously enough with Bülow and Berenhorst presenting their opposed interpretations of the factors which made for victory. Very soon afterwards Jomini and Clausewitz, each in his own way, rid themselves of "the ancients" and tried to penetrate the secret of Napoleonic warfare. Clausewitz in particular combined an understanding of strategy with a Berenhorst-like emphasis on moral factors. Philosopher as he was, he also sought to go much deeper and uncover the fundamentals of warfare by asking what it was and what it served for.

To Jomini, the secret was to be found in sophisticated maneuvering in accordance with a small number of fairly well defined, geometrically based, principles. Less interested in either geometry or maneuvering, Clausewitz before he started revising his work in 1827 put a much greater emphasis on the use of overwhelming force in order to smash the enemy main forces, after which the rest would be quite easy. Until about 1870, although Clausewitz's greatness was admitted and admired, Jomini was the more influential of the two. Then, after the victorious Moltke had pointed to Clausewitz as the greatest single influence on him, the wind shifted. Jomini was studied less, Clausewitz more often. This was true not only in Germany but in France where the military revival that started in the 1890s adopted him and du Picq to justify its emphasis on moral forces and its doctrine of the offensive at all costs. Whether or not these doctrines presented the "true" Clausewitz has often been debated. It is a question to which we shall return.

Meanwhile, it is probably correct to say that Jomini's name was not overlooked because he was outdated. To the contrary, it was because, like Lipsius before him, he had become so successful that his ideas on large-scale conventional warfare were considered the core business of strategy and taken very much for granted. Both Moltke and Schlieffen were, in one sense, his disciples. They employed his terminology but did no more than adapt it to their purposes. Moltke's most important contributions were to make the switch from internal to external lines and to adapt the Swiss general's doctrines to the new technologies represented by the railway and the telegraph. In fact, if my understanding of Moltke is correct, it was the introduction of those new technologies that forced him to make the switch.

Schlieffen was even less original. In essence all he did was to present a much simplified, uni-dimensional version of Jomini's thought. He limited it to enveloping operations and combined it with what, rightly or not, he saw as Clausewitz's unrelenting emphasis on the need for a single, climactic, annihilating battle.

Jomini's influence did not end in 1914. And it could be reasonably argued that as long as large armies go to war against each other in two-dimensional space, utilizing communications of every sort, and maneuvering among all kinds of natural and artificial obstacles, it is his work which will continue to provide the best guide of all.

6. WAR AT SEA

I n our survey so far, naval warfare has barely been mentioned. This is not because the role it played in war was unimportant. After all, from the Peloponnesian and the Punic Wars to the wars of the Napoleonic era, ships and navies had often figured prominently, sometimes even decisively. Not only had naval warfare always been a highly complex and technical subject, but the ancient Greeks clearly recognized the importance of *thessalocratia* (command of the sea). Nevertheless, navies were never made the subject of any major theoretical treatises.

To be sure, several authors either appended chapters on naval warfare to their works or had others do so, as Vegetius and Jomini e.g. did. With Vegetius the discussion of naval theory consists of a single page about the importance of having a navy always ready. To this were appended eight short chapters on the principles of building ships, navigating them, and fighting them. To Jomini ships were merely an aid to the movements of armies. What he has to say about them is completely unremarkable. As to Sun Tzu and Clausewitz, the greatest writers of all, judging by their published works one would think they did not even know that such a thing as the sea existed.

In the study of history, room must be allowed for accident. The first staff colleges were founded in Prussia and France from about 1770 on. Having discovered strategy as the most important subject they could teach, they began to flourish after 1815 and even more after 1871 when every important army in the world felt impelled to have one. Navies, however, remained backward. It was not until 1885 that an American, Commodore Stephen B. Luce, was able to persuade his country's Navy Department to set up a Naval War College at Newport, Rhode Island. Even then keeping it open and functioning was an uphill struggle. After two officers had turned down the job, Luce chose a forty-five-year-old naval captain of no great distinction, Alfred Mahan, to act as chief instructor. Mahan was the son of a well-known professor at West Point, Dennis Mahan. He had also written a volume called *The Navy in the Civil War, The Gulf and Inland Waters.* With that, though, his qualifications ended.

If a death sentence is said to "wonderfully concentrate the mind," so—in the case of some people at any rate—does the requirement to stand in front of a class and teach. Mahan taught class from 1886 to 1889. In 1890 he published his lectures in the form of a two-volume work, *The Influence of Seapower upon History, 1660–1783.* It was an immense success, probably selling more copies than all its predecessors put together (e.g. the first edition of Clausewitz only comprised 500 copies) and earning its author fame not only in the U.S but in Britain and Germany. The Kaiser himself was said to have kept it at his bedside, and made sure every naval officer read it. This success in turn was due to the fact that, in an age dominated by several great and would-be great "World Powers," Mahan had succeeded in putting together a remarkably coherent case as to why such Powers should have navies; what having such navies entailed; and how they should be used.

The book's main message is contained in the first and last chapters. Most of what is in between simply serves to illustrate how naval power had been successfully applied by the most important naval country of all, i.e. Britain. Its main concern was strategy. Convinced that continuing technological progress must soon render the details of building ships, arming them, sailing them, and fighting them obsolete, Mahan chose not to elaborate on those subjects. Strategy, on the other hand, was concerned with such questions as "the proper function of the navy in war; its true objective; the point or points upon which it should be concentrated; the establishment of depots of coal and supplies; the maintenance of communications between those depots and the home base; the military value of commerce-destroying as a decisive or secondary operation of war; [and] the system upon which commerce-destroying can be most efficiently conducted." In common with many other nineteenth century theorists Mahan believed that it could be reduced to a small number of principles. Concerning those principles, history had a great deal to say.

Describing his own intellectual development, Mahan says that he had first been led to reflect upon these questions while reading Mommsen's account of the critical role played by sea power during the Punic Wars. Not having control of the sea, the Carthaginian Navy had been reduced to operating mainly in home waters. Beyond that it could do no more than mount occasional raids and forays. Specifically, Carthage had been unable either to reinforce Hannibal's Italian campaign—which, in spite of its commander's genius, was thereby doomed to fail—or help its principal ally in Sicily, Syracuse. Rome, on the other hand, was able to use its command of the sea to cut Hannibal off from his bases in Africa and Spain (the overland route from the latter to Italy through the Alps being perilous, and most of the time, blocked by the Romans). It could also ship its own legions to both Spain and Sicily unhindered, keep King Philip V of Macedonia out of the war, and finally invade Africa itself. Thus seapower had helped shape the conduct of the war from beginning to end. It had also played a crucial part in Rome's victory.

In this as in so many subsequent wars, the importance of the sea consisted in that it served as a great highway by which men, armies, and goods could be transported more efficiently and more cheaply than by land. In both war and peace, the side able to do so enjoyed a critical advantage over the one who could not. Never more so than in the late nineteenth century when so much of every advanced nation's wealth had come to depend on its ability to export its industrial products while importing food and raw materials to feed its population and keep its factories running. During wartime, ensuring passage for one's own side while denying it to one's opponent was the function of the navy. Otherwise put, the navy of a great power—like almost all nineteenth century military theorists except for du Picq, Mahan was interested in none but great powers—found itself confronted by a double task, a negative one and a positive one. The negative part consisted of halting and destroying the enemy's commerce. The positive one, of making sure that one's own ships got through to their destinations.

In carrying out this double mission, two strategies presented themselves. One was to protect one's own shipping by providing them with escorts while simultaneously going after the enemy's cargo-bearing vessels. That strategy was known as *guerre de course* and was often resorted to by past belligerents. The other was to build up as powerful a battle-fleet as possible and use it to seek out, and defeat, the other side's navy. With "command of the sea" thus achieved, protecting one's own commerce while sweeping the enemy's remaining ships off the sea and blockading them in their ports would be relatively easy.

In other words, not for Mahan either war on commerce or its converse, escorted convoys. Both constituted half-hearted solutions and merely led to the dispersal of forces. Instead one should seek, and achieve, command of the sea, which Mahan treated almost as if it were some piece of country that could be conquered and ruled. At this point the similarity between Mahan and Clausewitz, at any rate the early Clausewitz before he started thinking of limited war, becomes obvious. Though he never mentions the Prussian general, our American born and bred prophet of seapower might have said that the best naval strategy was always to be very strong. First in general and then at the decisive point. Once created, the battle-fleet should be kept as concentrated as circumstances permitted and launched straight at the opposing fleet with the objective of annihilating it. Thus considered, Mahan's work represents one long diatribe against commerce-raiding (as well as the minor vessels by which, on the whole, it is carried out) and in favor of navies made up of the most powerful available capital ships.

Needless to say, this also entailed massive investments in other components of naval infrastructure such as qualified manpower, ports, depots, dry-docks, shipyards, factories for manufacturing arms and armor, and transportation facilities like the Suez, Panama and Kiel Canals. All of this Mahan explains at some length, which in turn contributed to his popularity, not only in naval circles, but among certain segments of industry and the political world as well.

As already mentioned, in setting forth his views Mahan had drawn mainly on what he interpreted as the historical experience of the strongest modern naval Power of all, i.e. Britain. Always tending to be pragmatic, though, the British had never been among the great producers of military theory, naval theory included. It was only a decade and a half after Luce had opened the US Naval War College that a similar reform could be carried through the British Navy. Even then many officers continued to argue that, in view of the Navy's past record, a theoretical education was not really needed. It is therefore not surprising that the introduction to the work of the next important naval author whom we must consider here, Julian Corbett, had much to say on the importance of military theory as such. To him, it was "a process by which we co-ordinate our ideas, define the meaning of the words we use, grasp the difference between essential and unessential factors, and fix and expose the fundamental data on which everyone is agreed. In this way we prepare the apparatus of practical discussion…. Without such an apparatus no two men can even think on the same line; much less can they ever hope to detach the real point of difference that divides them and isolate it for quiet solution." Achieving common ground was all the more essential in the case of an Empire, such as a British one, whose strategy would be made not by a single person or group at a single place but in innumerable conferences held at different places all around the world.

To be taught their own trade by a civilian—Corbett was a lawyer, but being a man of independent means he did not practice his profession and wrote full time—was regarded by many naval officers as an affront. As one of them wrote, Mr. Corbett had "permitted himself the indulgence of offering his audience his own views on the correctness or otherwise of the strategy adopted by naval officers in the past. His audience had usually treated his amateur excursions into the subject good-naturedly. Nevertheless his presumption has been resented, and he has apparently been deaf to the polite hints thrown out to him." Had they been able to foresee the contents of his most important theoretical work, *Some Principles of Maritime Strategy*, which came out in 1911, no doubt they would have been doubly offended.

If only because he had no true forerunners, Mahan's heroes were figures such as Colbert, who working for Louis XIV had created the modern French Navy, and Nelson, who more than anybody else had implemented the strategy of the decisive battle. By contrast, Corbett followed good approved late-nineteenth century practice in that he harnessed Clausewitz and Jomini to his cause. From the former he took the idea that naval warfare, like war as a whole, was merely a continuation of politics by other means. Jomini, Clausewitz's "great contemporary and rival," was said to have "entirely endorsed this view."

Having thus pulled down naval warfare down a peg—focusing on the fleet, Mahan had written almost as if policy did not exist—Corbett proceeded to explain that, on the whole, "men live upon land and not upon the sea." As a result, warfare in the latter was less important, and less decisive, than that which took place on the former. History could count many wars which had been decided purely on land without any reference to operations at sea. But the reverse was not true. That even applied to the Second Punic War, which Mahan had used as his starting point and case-study *par excellence*.

In their more mature days, both Clausewitz and Jomini had concluded that offensive war *à outrance* was only one form of war and that policy might dictate the use of other, more circumscribed methods. The latter had also shown, in considerable detail, how maneuvers by widely *dispersed* forces could lead to interesting strategic combinations and result in victory. Add the fact that, at sea as on land, the defensive was the more powerful form of war, and Mahan's prescription for using the concentrated fleet for seeking out the enemy and dealing a single offensive blow turned out to be completely wrong. Instead, and other things being equal, a compelling case could be made in favor of a careful, and necessarily prolonged, struggle of attrition—safeguarding one's own commerce, disrupting that of the enemy by every means that came to hand, and using the Navy to land forces at selected points in the enemy's rear so as to disrupt his plans and throw him out of gear. All this was particularly true if the political entity waging the war was not a country facing a neighbor but a far-flung empire dependent on its lines of communication.

A much better historian than Mahan, Corbett was able to support his argument by means of detailed case-studies. The most comprehensive of those was *England in the Seven Years War*, published in 1907 specifically to refute Mahan and quickly getting into the "limitations of naval action." Acting on a grand design thought out by the Elder Pitt, most of the time the British had *not* attempted to seek out the main French fleet and bring it to battle. Instead they had striven to contain the enemy and limit his movements; all the while protecting their own commerce and using their superior sea-power to assist their allies and grab prizes, such as India and Quebec, as came their way. The result of this "combined strategy" might not be decisive in the sense aimed at by Mahan. Though many combats took place, no general action between the two fleets was ever fought. When the War ended, so far were the British from achieving complete command of the sea that French commerce raiding still continued. The main French fleet also remained in being. The Peace of Paris, though achieved by strangulation rather than by some smashing victory, was "the most triumphant we ever made." It marked a critical step on Britain's way to world Empire.

Compared to those who came before and after them, Mahan and Corbett were giants. Blunt and to the point, the former can justly claim to have been the first writer who spelled out a comprehensive theory of naval warfare, a subject which hitherto had either been treated as secondary or neglected altogether. Highly sophisticated and tending towards understatement, the latter served as a useful corrective by emphasizing the limitations of maritime strategy and pointing out that command of the sea might be extremely useful even if it was not brought about by a climactic battle between the concentrated fleets of both sides; and even if, as a result, it was not as absolute as Mahan would have wished. The unique stature enjoyed by both authors has much to do with the fact that, instead of contenting themselves with the technical aspects of ports, navigation, ships and weapons, they started from first principles. The former looked into the objectives of naval warfare *per se*. The latter linked it to policy which might be less limited or more.

With these two approaches to naval warfare in front of them, it would almost be true to say that subsequent theorists were left with little more than crumbs to argue about. As new technological devices such as the submarine and the aircraft joined naval warfare some believed that Mahan had thereby been rendered obsolete. As two world wars showed, the introduction of submarines made commerce-raiding into a much more formidable proposition. On the other hand, aircraft threatened to take command of the sea away from ships, or at least to prevent fleets from approaching close to the land and thus making it much harder for them to force their opponents into battle. The Mahanist response, naturally enough, was to use aircraft in order to combat submarines and put at least some of them on board ships. By doing so they greatly increased the power of the capital ship and the range at which it was able to bring its weapons to bear and, as Mahan's followers claimed, turned command of the sea into a much more viable proposition than Mahan himself could have ever dreamed.

At the beginning of the twenty-first century, both schools are alive and well, though it must be admitted that the debate has become some-what academic. Command of the sea in the grand style, implying oper-ations that stretch across entire oceans, is now an objective sought after by one country only. Over the last fifty years, even that country has wit-nessed the number of its aircraft carriers, as the vital components in that command, dwindle from just under 100 (including escorts) to a mere 11. Whether for economic or geographical reasons, virtually all the rest have given up their capital ships. Without exception, what carriers they have are decidedly second-rate. In the process they reduced their navies to little more than coast-guards, which are incapable of independent operations far from home.

The age of global warfare, which opened in the final decades of the seventeenth century (not accidentally, the period in which both Mahan and Corbett open their detailed historical studies) appears to have ended in 1945. It was definitely buried in 1991 when the Soviet Union col-lapsed, taking the Red Navy with it. Thereby leaving, one hopes and fears, precious little meat for naval theorists to sink their teeth into concerning the future of war at sea.

7. THE INTERWAR PERIOD

T HROUGHOUT history, all too often the end of an armed conflict has served as a prelude to the next one. Never was this more true than at the end of World War I. Though it was sometimes described as "the war to end all wars," all it did was provide a temporary respite. Scarcely had the guns fallen silent when people started looking into the future on the assumption that the Great Powers had not yet finished fighting each other. This naturally gave rise to the question, how would the next war be waged?

To virtually all of those who tried, the point of departure was the need to minimize casualties. True to its name, the Great War had been fought with greater ferocity, and resulted in more dead and injured, than many of its predecessors put together. Confirming the predictions of some pre-war writers, such as the Jewish-Polish banker Ivan Bloch, this was the direct result of the superiority of the defense as brought about by modern firepower. Hence the most pressing problem was to find ways to bypass, or overcome, that firepower and that defense. Failure to do so might render the next war as unprofitable as, in the eyes of many, the struggle of 1914–1918 had been. To say nothing of the possibility that the dreadful losses and destruction suffered might cause it to end in revolution, as had already occurred in Russia, Austria-Hungary, and Germany.

In any event, the first serious theoretical treatise designed to solve the problem was written by an Italian general, Giulio Douhet. An engineer by trade, during the early years of the century Douhet had become fascinated with the military possibilities of the internal combustion engine. A little later he was also found dabbling in futurist ideas concerning the spiritual qualities allegedly springing from those two speedy new vehicles, the motor car and the aircraft, claiming that they had the ability to rejuvenate the world and Italy in particular. As a staff officer in 1915–18, he was in a position to observe no fewer than *twelve* Italian offensives directed against the Austrians across the river Isonzo. All twelve failed, producing hundreds of thousands of casualties for little or no territorial gain. He imagined there had to be a better way of doing things. One of those, which he had already promoted during the war itself, was the creation of a massive bomber force to be used against the enemy. Douhet's masterpiece, *Il dominio del aereo* (Command of the Air) was published in 1921. Though it took time to be translated, a survey of the interwar military literature shows that its leading ideas were widely studied and debated.

To Douhet, then, "the form of any war ... depends upon the technical means of war available." In the past, firearms had revolutionized war. Next it was the turn of small caliber rapid fire guns, barbed wire and, at sea, the submarine. The most recent additions were the air arm and poison gas, both of them still in their infancy but with the potential to "completely upset all forms of war so far known." In particular, so long as war was fought only on the surface of the earth it was necessary for one side to break through the other's defenses in order to win. Those defenses, however, tended to become stronger and stronger until, in the conflict that had just ended, they had extended over practically the entire battlefield and barred the troops of both sides from moving forward. Behind the hard crusts presented by the fronts the populations of the various states carried on civilian life almost undisturbed. Mobilizing those populations, the states in question were able to produce the wherewithal of total war and sustain the struggle for years on end.

The advent of the aircraft was bringing this situation to an end. Capable of overflying both fronts and natural obstacles, and possessing a comparatively long range, aircraft would be used to attack civilian centers of population and industry. The air could be traversed in all directions with equal ease, nor was there a way to predict which target would be hit next. That was why no effective defense against such attacks was possible. Each attacking aircraft would have to be countered by twenty defensive ones; or else, if the job were entrusted to guns, hundreds if not thousands of them.

Extrapolating from the raids that had taken place in 1916–1918, Douhet showed that forty aircraft dropping eighty tons of bombs might have "completely destroyed" a city the size of Treviso, leaving alive "very few" of its 17,000 inhabitants. A mere three aircraft could deliver as much firepower as could a modern battleship in a single broadside, whereas a thousand aircraft could deliver ten times as much firepower as could the entire British Navy—counting 30 battleships—in ten. Yet the price-tag of a single battleship was said to be about equal to that of a thousand aircraft. To use modern terminology, the differential in cost/effectiveness between the two arms was little less than phenomenal. As Douhet pointed out, moreover, even these calculations failed to take account of the fact that the career of military aviation had just begun and that aircraft capable of lifting as much as ten tons each might soon be constructed.

Under such circumstances, investments in armies and navies would come to a gradual halt. The resources freed in this way should be diverted to the air arm, regarded as the decisive one in any future conflict. Properly used, it could bring about a quick decision—so quick, indeed, that there might scarcely be sufficient time for the two remaining ones to be mobilized and deployed. Given that the character of the new weapon was inherently offensive, most of the aircraft ought to be not fighters but bombers. Instead of forming part of the army and navy, as was then the case in all major armed forces except those of Britain, they should be assembled in an independent air force.

At the outbreak of the next war that air force should be launched like a shell from a cannon, mounting an all-out attack against the enemy's air bases with the objective of gaining "command of the air." Once command of the air had been attained—meaning that the enemy, his bases destroyed, was no longer able to interfere with operations—the attackers should switch from military objectives to civilian ones, knocking them out one by one. Industrial plants as well as population centers ought to be attacked; the attackers' principal weapon ought to be gas, the aim not merely to kill but to demoralize. Leaping over and ignoring the usual forces that defend a country, a war waged by such means might be over almost before it had begun. In so far as it would minimize the casualties of both the attacker and the defender (whose population, driven to the point of madness, would force the government to surrender) it also represented a more humane *modus operandi* than an endless struggle of attrition.

Like Mahan, to whom he owed much, Douhet has been accused of overstating his case. When the test came in World War II it was found that his calculations, made in terms of a uniform bomb pattern dropping on an area of 500 by 500 meters, did not allow for the practical difficulties of accurately landing ordnance on target. As a result, far more bombs and aircraft would be needed to obliterate a given objective than he thought. Perhaps because gas was not used, by and large the populations which found themselves at the receiving end of those bombs proved much more resilient than he had expected. This caused one critic to quip that Douhet could not be blamed for the fact that the people whom he used as the basis for his calculations were, after all, Italians, whom everyone knew to be lousy soldiers. Finally, once radar had been introduced the air-weapon turned out to be much better adapted for defensive purposes than its original prophet—he died in 1930—had foreseen. In the air, as on land, World War II developed into a prolonged and extremely deadly struggle of attrition.

Nevertheless, given that it is with the evolution of military thought that we are dealing here, it should be said at once that no other treatise written on the subject of air warfare has ever presented nearly as coherent a picture as did *Il dominio del aereo*, nor has any other treatise been nearly as influential. In part, this was for institutional reasons. Engaging in close air support (CAS) and interdicting enemy lines of communication were missions which might conceivably be undertaken by an army air force. But gaining command of the air and attacking the other side's homeland were clearly independent missions which called for an equally independent air force. Be this as it may, the mirage of dealing a rapid and all-powerful blow from the air—so rapid and so powerful that the need for the remaining armed forces would be all but obviated—has continued to fascinate airmen. It did so right through World War II and into the nuclear age when, but for the fact that nuclear weapons were too powerful to use, it might have been realized. Surrounded by an enormous number of publications which added little to Douhet's original vision, in 1988 it received its second most powerful formulation ever at the hands of an American officer, Colonel John A. Warden III.

To carry out the air-offensive he envisaged Douhet had proposed to rely on a comparatively small force made up of elite warriors, a vision which meshed well with the anti-democratic, fascist ideas that he also entertained. Much the same was true of the great prophet of mechanized warfare on land, the British general John Frederick Fuller. Born nine years after Douhet and destined to outlive him by more than thirty years (he died in 1966), Fuller was a self-taught intellectual whose interests ranged from Greek philosophy to Jewish mysticism or *Kabbalah*. As a young officer before World War I he had been much concerned to discover the principles of war, finally settling down on six. From the end of 1916 on he found himself acting as chief of staff to the Royal Tank Corps to whose organization and operations he made a critical contribution.

This is not the place to engage in a detailed examination of Fuller's intellectual development, a task that has been successfully undertaken by several other writers. Suffice it to say that, like so many others, he was appalled by the loss of life which had resulted from trench warfare during World War I. Like so many others he sought a solution, but unlike so many others he possessed one which had already been tried and applied to some extent. As Bloch had foreseen, the advent of magazine rifles, machine guns and quick-firing artillery had saturated the battlefield in a storm of steel, making offensive movement practically impossible. What, then, was more natural than to put a moving shield in front of the advancing troops? A shield capable of resisting the penetrating power of modern high velocity bullets and shrapnel was, however, likely to be heavy. Hence it should be provided with an engine and put on wheels or, better still, tracks.

As a serving soldier in France, Fuller was not involved with the early development of the tank which was the work of others. Later, having gained practical experience in planning armored forces and operating them, his decisive contribution was to demand, and to suggest ways for, the tank's transformation from a mechanized siege engine—its original purpose—into a modern version of the old heavy cavalry. To put it briefly, crossing trenches and breaking through the enemy's fortified system was one thing and one which, by the end of World War I, was being achieved fairly regularly both by the Germans, who relied on storm-trooper tactics, and by the Allies with the assistance of tanks. However, and as was proved *inter alia* by the Battle of Cambrai (which Fuller himself helped plan and direct) in November–December 1917, merely doing so was not enough. To bring about the enemy's collapse it was necessary to push deeper into his territory, attacking his vitals such as command posts and communications and depots and bringing about his collapse from the rear to the front. Tanks, not the early cumbersome machines but the more mobile ones that were becoming available towards the end of the war, were to play a vital role in this kind of operation. And so were mobile artillery and aircraft.

Fuller's famous Plan 1919 was intended to realize these ideas but came too late for it to be turned into practice. Once peace had been restored Fuller, while still in the army, became the principal exponent of mechanization. In numerous publications—he was a prolific writer who, however, often tended to overstate his case—he argued that war, like every other field of human life, was decisively affected by the progress of science. Like Douhet, he considered that currently the most important fruits of science were the internal combustion engine, on which depended the airplane and the tank, as well as poison gas. Whether armed forces liked it or not, these devices *had* to be employed because failure to do so was to risk being left behind. Future warfare on land would center on the tank and be based almost entirely on tracks as artillery, recce units, engineers, signals, supply, and maintenance all became mechanized. Once they had mechanized themselves armies would enjoy almost as much freedom of movement as did ships at sea. They would use it in order to maneuver against each other, concentrating against select sections of the enemy front, breaking through them, and bringing about victory at comparatively low cost.

While not alone in the field, Fuller did as much as anybody to stimulate the debate about tanks and mechanization. Coming as they did from the ex-chief of staff of the most advanced mechanized force in history, his views commanded particular respect. Barring the most extreme ones—e.g. the idea that armies should consist of tanks alone and that every infantryman should be provided with his individual tankette and use it to wage guerrilla warfare—many of his suggestions have come to pass. Indeed it could be argued that all modern mechanized armies stem from the experimental force which was first assembled on Salisbury Plain in 1928 and of which, had he wanted to, he could have been the commander. The problem was that, considering himself not merely a reformer but a philosopher, Fuller went on to surround himself with an immensely complicated network of intellectual propositions on the nature of war, life and history. Combining all these different strands, many of his historical writings were decidedly brilliant. But much of his theorizing was decidedly half-baked; so, for example, his idea that all things fell "naturally" into three parts.

In particular, Fuller, like Douhet, considered democracy and the mass-armies to which it had given rise from the time of the French Revolution to be harmful and degenerate. Also like Douhet, he hoped to replace those mass armies by a small force of elite, tank-riding, professional warriors. Not only would war thereby be conducted much more efficiently, but the example set by such a force would have a regenerating impact on, and serve as a model for, society as a whole. But whereas Douhet was in line with majority opinion in his own country and enjoyed the friendship of Benito Mussolini, Fuller, having resigned from the Army in 1928, did himself a lot of harm by joining the British Union of Fascists and writing articles in a Fascist vein. Later he even went to Germany as an official guest of Hitler's in order to attend the Wehrmacht's maneuvers.

In the history of twentieth century military thought, Fuller's name is almost always associated with that of his contemporary and friend, Basil Liddell Hart. Born in 1895, unlike Fuller, Liddell Hart was not a professional soldier but had studied history at Cambridge for one year. At that time he volunteered for service, received a commission, and was sent to fight in France. Gassed at the Somme, Captain (throughout his life he enjoyed emphasizing the military rank he had attained) Liddell Hart spent the rest of the War in Britain training infantrymen. It was in this capacity that he first started thinking seriously, and writing, about armed conflict. When the War ended, and having been invalided out of the army, he made his living as a sports journalist.

Concerning his intellectual development, two points are worth noting. First, like so many of his generation who, along with him, were educated in public schools, Liddell Hart was brought up on the notion that war was akin to sport and games. In his memoirs he relates, proudly, that he was rather good at football. Not because his coordination and technique were in any way outstanding, but because he could engage in various combinations and foresee where the ball was likely to end up. Second, and again like so many of his generation, Liddell Hart ended the War as a fervent admirer of the British military establishment which, after all, had just fought and won the greatest armed conflict in history until then. Within a few years he completely reversed himself, joining the then fashionable trend and becoming disillusioned with the War in general and with its conduct at the hand of the British High Command in particular. In criticizing that conduct, his experience as a popular journalist and interest in games were to come in handy.

Like Fuller, Liddell Hart arrived at the conclusion that sending men to attack frontally in the face of the machine guns which were trained at them had been the height of folly. All it did was lead to masses of unnecessary casualties. More than Fuller, he took care to trace this folly to its origin which, according to him, was to be found not in simple bloody-mindedness but in the writings of the greatest of all military philoso-phers, Carl von Clausewitz. He called Clausewitz the "Mahdi of Mass;" the prophet whose clarion-call had misled generations of officers into the belief that the best, indeed almost the only, way to wage war was to form the greatest possible concentration of men and weapons and launch it straight ahead against the enemy. In 1914–18 this "Prussian Marsel-laise" had borne its horrible fruit. The results could be seen on literally thousands of war memorials erected not only in Britain but all over the British Empire and, indeed, the world.

Like Fuller, Liddell Hart was largely self-taught. However, he en-joyed several advantages over the older man. For one thing he was less interested in the non-military aspects of history and philosophy. This caused his historical writings to be somewhat one-dimensional; not for him the scintillating synthesis of politics, economics, sociology, and cul-ture that often marks Fuller's work at its best. However, it also saved him from engaging in the kind of mystic flights that sometimes made Fuller appear incomprehensible if not unbalanced. He wrote clearly and to the point, and indeed cynics might argue that part of his success stemmed from the fact that his work was so simplistic even generals could under-stand it. By the time he set forth his ideas about Clausewitz in *The Ghost of Napoleon* (originally delivered as the Lees-Knowles lectures for 1933) he was already the most famous military journalist in Britain. By way of confirming his status, he was working for the *Encyclopaedia Britannica* as well. Four years earlier, in 1929, he had set forth his mature doctrines in *The Decisive Wars of History*. Expanded to include World War II and reprinted many times under such titles as *Strategy: The Indirect Approach* and *Strategy*, it was to become perhaps the most influential military study of the twentieth century.

Though he started his career as an infantry tactician, much like his predecessors from Jomini on Liddell Hart's main interest was strategy. Like them, this fact caused him to ignore the period from about 600 AD. (the wars of Belisarius and Narses) to 1500 AD. (the Franco-Italian Wars in Italy), a 900-year period apparently marked by nothing but endless skirmishing in which nothing of interest took place. For the rest, however, he accepted the late nineteenth century view, which Mahan, Douhet and Fuller had all shared, that whereas the forms of war were subject to change, its fundamental principles were not. In this way he was able to treat ancient and modern campaigns, starting with Alexander the Great and ending with Ludendorff in 1918, as if they were basically similar. He ironed out all differences between them and focused on what, to him, was the essential point. The essential point, arising straight out of the experience of World War I, was that direct attacks against the enemy's front had to be avoided at all cost since they inevitably ended in failure.

To restore the power of the offensive and save casualties, Liddell Hart went on to recommend "the indirect approach." Rather than attacking the enemy head on, he had to be weakened first by having his limbs cut off, his organization disrupted, and the mind of his commander unbalanced. As he sought to show at the hand of historical studies—in reality, little more than thumbnail sketches—this could be achieved by combining rapidity of movement with secrecy and surprise. The goal was to conceal the true center of gravity for as long as possible; the means were to be strikes carried out by dispersed forces coming from unexpected directions and following the route of least expectation. Even if mounting them meant overcoming topographical obstacles. Above all, every plan had to possess "two branches," which meant it should be drawn up in such a way as to keep Red guessing at Blue's true objectives. It should also be sufficiently flexible to enable that objective to be changed if, by some mishap, the first one turned out to be too strongly defended.

All these maneuvers were to be carried out in two dimensional space, along lines of communication, among all kinds of natural and artificial obstacles, while trailing "an umbilical cord of supply," and against an enemy who presumably was also capable of maneuvering. To this extent they owed a lot to Jomini, although it was characteristic of Liddell Hart that, in his *chef d'oeuvre*, his great predecessor's name is never mentioned. Consisting essentially of movement and characterized by means of colored arrows stretching across a map, war was presented almost as if it were some kind of sophisticated game played between opposing teams.

This was particularly true of his mature work. Having started his career as a trainer of infantry, the older Liddell Hart became the more pronounced in his tendency to give tactics a short shrift. Mobilization, logistics, command, communication and control, and those twin unimportant questions of killing and dying were also lightly skipped over. As he once wrote, "could one but remove the horrible suffering and mutilation it would be the finest purifier of nations ever known." Reading his last book, *A History of World War II*, one might be excused for thinking it was all about operational movement and very little else.

Having once overcome his early admiration for the British performance in World War I, during the early twenties Liddell Hart had also become interested in mechanization. In this field his mentor was Fuller whom he had known since 1920; and indeed so much did the younger man lift, not to say, steal, from the works of the older one that their friendship almost went to the dogs. Liddell Hart's vision of mechanized armed forces was set forth in *Paris, or the Future of War* (1925) as well as *The Remaking of Modern Armies* (1927). In those small but extremely well-written studies he talked about the novel combination of tanks, aircraft, and poison gas as weapons. With their aid the defense could be skipped over or overcome, stalemate broken "within a few hours, or at most days." And the war brought to a swift and cheap, if violent, end.

The main characteristics of both land-borne mechanized vehicles and aircraft were speed and flexibility. One might have thought that Liddell Hart would have seized upon them as the ideal tools with which to implement a strategy of indirect approach against opposing and equally mobile armed forces. Instead, however, he was enticed by a Douhet-like vision of "London, Manchester, Birmingham and half a dozen other great centers simultaneously attacked, the business localities and Fleet Street wrecked, Whitehall a heap of ruins, the slum districts maddened into the impulse to break loose and maraud, the railways cut, factories destroyed." As a result, he never quite came around to forging the missing link between the two halves of his vision, the strategic and the technological. Though *Paris* does contain a few brilliant lines about that problem, in *The Decisive Wars of History* the entire question of mechanization is barely mentioned.

What prevented Liddell Hart from making a detailed forecast of the *Blitzkrieg*, with its characteristic armored divisions made up of different arms, was his abiding revulsion with the horrors of World War I and his determination, which he shared with so many of his generation, that they should not be repeated. From about 1931 on this caused him to switch from attempts to devise more effective ways to win towards thinking about less costly ways to avoid defeat. Following Corbett—once again, without mentioning him by name—he now claimed that the "British Way in Warfare" had always been to stay out of massive continental commitments. Instead it had relied on its navy to keep the enemy at bay (and harass and weaken him by means of well-directed strokes at selected points) and on continental allies to deliver the *coup de main*.

By 1939 he had convinced himself that "the dominant lesson from the experience of land warfare, for more than a generation past, has been the superiority of the defense over attack." Even in the air, as experience in Spain had shown, "the prospects of the defense are improving." Therefore, instead of Britain repeating its World War I error which had led to so many casualties, it could safely trust the "dauntless" French to stop the Germans. Britain itself, its armed forces thoroughly modernized and mechanized, should revert to its traditional strategy, relying primarily on blockade on the one hand and airpower on the other. This had the additional advantage that it would make universal conscription and mass armies unnecessary—a preference for small professional forces being one thing which Liddell Hart, who unlike the other two was not a fascist but a liberal, shared with them.

Followed, as they were, by the smashing success of the early *Blitzkrieg* offensives, these predictions all but discredited Liddell Hart. By the middle of World War II he was regarded almost as *passé*. The means, kosher and not so kosher, by which he revived his reputation after 1945 and presented himself as the person who had taught the Germans all they knew need not concern us here. Suffice it to say that all three thinkers discussed in this chapter so far started from the idea that World War I had provided an example of how *not* to do things. All three were shocked by the number of casualties which had been brought about by the power of the defense. To all three, that power was not the natural result of modern technology (including logistics, a subject to which none of them paid much attention) but, on the contrary, of a failure to make use of its most recent possibilities; whether in the air, or on the ground, or both. Each in his own way, all three sought to discover ways by which comparatively small, but modern, armed forces could overcome that defense so as to once again make it possible to wage war quickly and decisively. Although, as has just been explained, Liddell Hart ended up by retreating from that proposition.

Compared to Douhet, Fuller, and Liddell Hart, Erich Ludendorff was a towering figure. Much more than the former two he understood what modern war was like at the top. Unlike the last-named he did not regard it as some kind of field game. As he wrote, having lost two sons, "the war has spared me nothing." On the other hand, and again unlike

Liddell Hart in particular, neither did he shrink from its horrors. Ludendorff's post-war dabbling with anti-Semitism, anti-Catholicism, and anti-freemasonry (he could never make up his mind which of the three international forces posed the greater danger to Germany) bordered on the paranoid and has been rightly condemned. However, this should not be allowed to obscure the fact that his vision of future armed conflict was awesome and, which is more important, more nearly correct than any of the rest.

Having spent over two years in charge of the war effort of the most powerful belligerent in history until then, Ludendorff did not believe that a first class modern state could be brought to its knees rapidly and cheaply by aircraft dropping bombs on its civilian population. Nor could this be achieved by fleets of tanks engaging in mobile operations, however indirect and however brilliant. In part, Ludendorff merely continued the work of some pre-1914 militarist writers, such as Colmar von der Goltz and Theodor von Bernhardi, who had advocated total mobilization and mass armies. Up to a point, too, *Der Totale Krieg* (*The Nation at War*) both recounted his own experience and, by attacking many of his less cooperative colleagues, sought to explain why Germany, with himself at its head, had lost the war.

Whatever the book's precise origins and purpose, Ludendorff's main thesis was that the developing technologies of production, transportation and communication made modern war into much more than merely a question of armed forces maneuvering against each other for mastery of some battlefield. Instead it was "total"—the title of his book—basing itself on all the forces of the nation, and requiring that the latter be mobilized to the last person and the last screw.

To be sure, the next war would make use of all available modern weapons, including poison gas. Civilians as well as the armed forces would be targeted, and the resulting number of casualties, destruction, and suffering would be immense. Even more important than the mobilization of material resources was the spiritual mobilization of the people; a point concerning which Ludendorff felt Imperial Germany, with its old-fashioned authoritarian system of government and its neglect of the working classes, had been sadly deficient. The implication of such mobilization was an end to democracy and the liberties it entailed, including not only freedom of the press but of capitalist enterprise as well. For either industrialists or union leaders (during the War Ludendorff had had his troubles with both) to insist on their own privilege was intolerable. They, as well as the entire financial apparatus available to the state, were to be subjected to a military dictatorship. Nor was Ludendorff under any illusion that the nation's spiritual and material mobilization could be quickly improvised. Hence the dictatorship which he demanded, and for which he no doubt regarded himself as the most suitable candidate, was to be set up in peacetime and made permanent.

The next war would not be a gentlemanly fight for limited stakes to be won by the side with the swiftest and sharpest sword. Instead it would be a life and death struggle to be won by the belligerent with the greatest resources and the strongest willpower—which incidentally disposed of any childish illusions concerning small, professional and highly mobile, let alone chivalrous, armed forces. Anything not serving the war effort would have to be ruthlessly discarded, and this specifically included playing at politics. The latter would, in effect, be swallowed by the war; they would become identical with it. "All the theories of Clausewitz should be thrown overboard.... Both war and policy serve the existence of the nation. However, war is the highest expression of the people's will to live. Therefore politics must be made subordinate to war." Or, to the extent that they were not, they were superfluous and, indeed, treasonable.

After 1945 Ludendorff's military thought was often attacked by featherweight commentators. In addition to taking a justified dislike to his racism and his early support for Hitler, they mistook their world, in which nuclear weapons had made total warfare as he understood it impossible, for his. During these years it was Liddell Hart and Fuller who, whether rightly or not, were celebrated as the fathers of the *Blitzkrieg*. Nevertheless the fact remains that it was not their vision of World War II but Ludendorff's which turned out to be only too horribly true.

To be sure, fleets of aircraft did fly over the fronts and bombed cities on a scale which, had he only been able to envisage it, might have made even Ludendorff blanch. Ground-support aircraft, cooperating more closely with the tanks, helped carry out spectacular mobile operations on the ground. The combination of aircraft, armor, and wireless restored operational mobility, and laid the groundwork for smashing victories in which countries the size of Poland and France were conquered with previously unimaginable speed. It also did much to re-establish the balance between defense and offense, although events were to show that both tanks and aircraft (the latter, thanks to the introduction of radar) were as capable of operating on the defense, and preventing a breakthrough, as they were of helping it to take place.

Where Ludendorff proved most correct, however, was in insisting that the next major war would be broadly like the last. Like its predecessor, it would develop into a gigantic struggle and a prolonged one. It would both demand and make possible the mobilization of all resources under a regime which, even in democratic countries, came pretty close to doing away with politics while putting everyone and everything under its own control; in 1945 the British Ministry of Food alone had no fewer than 30,000 employees.

Ludendorff's posthumous triumph may be seen in the fact that, by the time World War II was over, a continent had been devastated and between forty and sixty million people lay dead. As the coming decades were to prove, the history of conventional military theory had run its course.

8. 1945 TO THE PRESENT

THE fact that World War II had effectively put an end to conventional military theory was not evident at first. During the decades that followed a great many attempts were made to continue the debate, sometimes by men (there appear to be few if any women in the field) who had already made their mark before 1939. Enormous numbers of publications were produced and, almost as rapidly, forgotten. Of their authors none attained the prominence of a Fuller, let alone a Liddell Hart.

The paucity of first-rate theory is not difficult to explain. When the Gulf War broke out in 1991, forty-six years after Hiroshima, by far the most important motive power was still the internal combustion engine including, of course, jets. By far the most important formations were still those old and trusted World War products, i.e. squadrons of fighter bombers, armored divisions, and, at sea, task-forces centering around aircraft carriers and intended to achieve command of the sea (although, as it turned out, there was no one with whom to dispute it). As both fighter bombers and armored divisions operated by dropping or firing massive quantities of steel into the air they were heavily dependent on lines of communications for that steel as well as fuel; with the result that the objective of strategy remained, as it had been from the days of von Bülow and Jomini on, to cut those lines.

To be sure, the forces were festooned with a great many other weapons and, as fashionable modern parlance has it, weapon systems. Missiles and cruise missiles and remotely piloted vehicles and helicopters; computers and data-links and satellites and global positioning systems; all these and more were employed. When everything was said and done, however, none proved capable of making the campaign very different from what, say, the German invasion of Poland in 1939 had been.

Between 1945 and 1991, faced with what was usually understood as unprecedented technological progress many, perhaps the majority, of writers focused their efforts on the ways new weapons would be integrated into future war and influence its shape. Thus, in the fifties and sixties, it was often a question of coming to terms with the short and medium range missiles then coming into service (inter-continental missiles with their nuclear warheads are a different story and will be dealt with below). Later the 1973 Arab-Israeli War, which at the time was the most modern of its kind, led to a lively debate concerning the relative merits of armor and anti-tank missiles; airpower and anti-aircraft defenses; attack and defense; and quality versus quantity. Spurred by America's failure in Vietnam, which was blamed on the strategy of attrition adopted by the US armed forces, the 1980s saw a revival of conventional warfare theory centering on such ideas as maneuver warfare and AirLand Battle. As their names imply, both focused on strategy and the operational art while all but ignoring grand strategy. The first took the German campaigns of World War II as its model, so much so that, for some ten years, "German" and "excellent" were considered synonymous and ex-Wehrmacht generals were treated to free lunches at the Pentagon. The second could barely be distinguished from, say, what Patton and his supporting XIXth Tactical Air Command had done to the Wehrmacht at Falaise in 1944.

Throughout this period, very great attention was naturally devoted to Soviet military theory and doctrine. As both they and their opponents in the Cold War never tired of pointing out, the Soviets had inherited from Karl Marx the idea that war was not only a military struggle. It was instead a socio-economic phenomenon to be considered "in its entirety," though exactly what this meant when it came to working out the details was not always clear. During the twenties and thirties Soviet authors such as Tuchachevsky seem to have drawn on their own experience in the Civil War and Soviet-Polish War, in which there had been a considerable amount of operational movement carried out by cavalry corps. With Fuller acting as the stimulant, mobility was married to mechanization. The outcome was something known as "the battle in depth;" meaning a highly offensive campaign which would be launched not merely along the front but against the enemy's communications, depots, and command centers as well. Moreover, as Marxists the Soviets professed to have as much faith in "the people" as Fuller and Douhet had been skeptical of them. If only for that reason, unlike their Western counterparts they never surrendered to the siren-song of small, elite, armed forces.

Shortly after the Battle of Moscow in 1941–42, i.e. at a time in which the Soviet Union had just collected itself from its initial defeats and begun to wage total war like no other country in history, Stalin promulgated the "five permanently operating factors." Not surprisingly they bore a strong family resemblance to the picture painted by Ludendorff six years previously—even to the point where one commentator claimed that the German general's doctrine was also capable of being summed up in five points. The most important factor was the political stability of the homeland, a phrase which, coming from under *that* particular moustache, might well make one shudder. This was followed by the morale of the armed forces, the quality and quantity of their divisions, armament, and the commanders' capacity for organizing the resources at their disposal. From then until the end of the Cold War, it was claimed that the best way to annihilate the enemy was by means of massive armored offensives. Much like, say, the ones which the Red Army had mounted against the Germans in 1943–45, only deeper, more powerful, and better.

Over the decades, these debates provided a living for thousands if not tens of thousands of analysts in- and out of uniform. More important, on both sides of the Iron Curtain they fed vast "military-industrial complexes" which gave employment to millions and were not without influence both on the economies and on the political systems of the countries which they were supposed to serve. Overshadowing them all, however, was the question of nuclear weapons. The first atomic bomb dropped on Hiroshima was some fifteen hundred times as powerful as the largest weapon in existence until then. With the advent of hydrogen bombs the gap widened still further; but even when much smaller tactical nuclear weapons appeared on the scene the discrepancy between the two kinds of arms remained immense. In any attempt to understand the nature of future war and the way in which it should be conducted, the altogether unprecedented challenges posed by nuclear weapons have to be addressed first. Failure to do so was like discussing the activities of toddlers throwing pebbles at each other while the adults, machine guns at the ready, stood by and watched.

In any case, the true significance of nuclear weapons was not understood at first. In part this was because there were not too many of them around. Nor was it certain that the relatively few and slow bombers capable of carrying them would necessarily arrive at their targets. Hence it was excusable that many, though not all, senior politicians and military men in the West believed that the next war would be much like the last one, give or take a number of cities turned into radioactive wastes. In 1947, Stalin's above-mentioned picture of total war was re-issued specifically with this message in mind. In the face of the American nuclear monopoly of the time, it had to be shown that "adventurist" ideas could not succeed since other factors were even more decisive.

Previously, whenever some new and powerful weapon appeared on the scene it had only been a question of time before it became fully incorporated into military doctrine and, as had happened e.g. to the tank and the aircraft carrier, was turned into the latter's mainstay. From the late forties on strenuous attempts were made to treat nuclear arms in the same manner, i.e. devise ways for using them in war. First it was the USAF which, with its own interests as the sole organization capable of delivering the bomb to target very much in mind, pressed for its adoption as the mainstay of American and Western defense. Doing so, it came up with such aptly-named operations as "Bushwhacker," "Dropshot," and "Broiler." Later the idea of "Massive Retaliation" was adopted by the incoming Eisenhower Administration. As Secretary of State John Foster Dulles declared in a famous speech, the US would not permit the other side to dictate the site and mode of the next war. Instead, any attempt by the Communists to engage in aggression anywhere in the world *might* be instantly met with means, and at a place, of America's own choosing.

By the time it was made, the credibility of this threat was already in some doubt. In September 1949 the Soviet Union had detonated its first bomb. By the early fifties its arsenal, though still smaller than that of the US, was growing. Given that the US was the first to develop operational H bombs, possessed far more delivery vehicles, and had deployed those delivery vehicles across a worldwide chain of bases it could probably have "won" a nuclear exchange. Still this did not address the question as to what would happen if, in the face of an all-out American offensive, a few Soviet bombs somehow survived in their hideouts and, loaded aboard equally few bombers, found their way to North American targets such as New York and Washington D.C. Then as now, the Dr. Strangeloves of this world tried to exorcise the "bugaboo of radiation" and reassure the public that recovery from a nuclear war was possible. Then as now, the question proved unanswerable.

In the late fifties the situation changed again. Soviet nuclear power was growing, and so were the range and effectiveness of its delivery vehicles in the form of the first Intercontinental Ballistic Missiles (ICBM). The debate surrounding the concept of Massive Retaliation was replaced, or supplemented, by the question as to how the US itself could be protected against nuclear attack; leading to the emergence of city-busting and counter force, first strike and second strike. A broad consensus was formed that, precisely since cities could not be protected against a nuclear offensive, it was vital to have forces in place which could survive such an attack and still retaliate with sufficient force to wipe the other side off the map. The outcome was the famous Triad, a vast array of airborne, seaborne, and land-based nuclear strike forces linked together by an electronic command system and supposedly capable of "riding out" anything that the Soviet Union could throw at them. Perhaps because the 1962 Missile Crisis had given people a fright, over time the Triad's role in fighting a war tended to be de-emphasized and its deterrent function was given greater prominence. Projected onto the other side, which in spite of its occasional protests to the contrary was supposed to share the same objective, this doctrine became known as Mutual Assured Destruction or MAD.

A point to be made about these and other Western theories of nuclear power and its use in war is that, contrary to the vast majority of their predecessors, they were produced neither by serving commanders nor by retired ones. To be sure, it was the generals who were left in charge of the armed forces themselves; building them, organizing them, and training them for action. From time to time one uniformed figure or another would also put his voice into the debate by penning an article or, less often, a book. Still it was not they but civilian analysts—working either in the universities or, increasingly, so-called think-tanks especially created for the purpose—who produced the most important "strategic" volumes of the Cold War era, such as Albert Wohlstetter's *Selection and Use of Strategic Air Bases* (1954), William Kaufman's *Military Policy and National Security* (1956), Henry Kissinger's *Nuclear Weapons and Foreign Policy* (1957), Robert Osgood's *Limited War*, Herman Kahn's *On Thermonuclear War* (1960), and, above all, Thomas Schelling's *Arms and Influence* (1966).

Though ostensibly dealing with "strategy," all these works were concerned at least as much with deterring war as with devising better ways to fight it. As the title suggests, the last-named in particular all but renounced the use of armed force as suicidal. Instead it explained how a state might avail itself of nuclear arsenal to exercise diplomatic pressure on its opponent while itself resisting similar pressure. It was as if war itself had been cut down to size. To misuse a phrase coined by an earlier head of state, in the face of weapons literally capable of destroying the earth it had become too dangerous to leave to the generals.

From time to time, the question whether the balance of terror might not be upset, and a capability for at least limited war-fighting restored, by devising some kind of defensive umbrella was raised. As early as October 1945 a Canadian general went on record as saying that the means for countering the atomic bomb were "clearly in sight"—a premature statement, no doubt, but one which has since then been repeated countless times. In the late fifties communities and people were encouraged to provide themselves with anti-nuclear shelters and advertisements for such shelters, looking just like the typical American living room magically transported underground, were circulated. The late sixties brought ABM, or Anti-Ballistic Missiles. The idea was to "hit a bullet with a bullet," as the phrase went, and intercept the incoming Soviet missiles while still *en route*. The advent of MIRV, on which more below, terminated those hopes. In 1972 it led to the Strategic Arms Limitation Treaty which obliged both sides not to deploy Anti-Ballistic Missiles; however, in 1983, President Reagan's so-called Star Wars initiative once again aimed at rendering ballistic missiles "impotent and obsolete."

Reagan's Star War Initiative was followed by the Strategic Defense Initiative. So far it has resulted in a small number of launchers stationed in Alaska. Since testing under operational conditions is all but impossible, just how well it will work under a serious attack nobody knows. Each time tens of billions of dollars were sunk into the effort. Each time, it turned out that anything even resembling "reliable" protection was out of reach. Not, perhaps, because it could not be done from a technical point of view. But because, set in the context of nuclear weapons which are quite capable of annihilating entire societies in a second, "protection" and "reliable" constituted an oxymoron.

Running in parallel with the attempts to design a defense was the progressive introduction of smaller "tactical" nuclear weapons. Capable of being carried by a variety of delivery vehicles—from fighter bombers down to atomic bazookas—they raised the question whether they might not be used against at least some targets without running the risk of blowing up the world. Whether, in other words, nuclear warfare once it had broken out could not be contained within a single theater. Towards the late sixties the same question was raised with even greater urgency by the near-simultaneous appearance of two new technologies, MIRV (Multiple Independent Reentry Vehicles) and cruise missiles. Besides putting an end to any hope that incoming missiles might be intercepted—given that each missile was now made to carry as many as ten warheads—both MIRV and cruise missiles were capable of delivering those warheads with unprecedented accuracy, "straight through Mr. Brezhnev's window." Both therefore gave rise to hopes, if that is the word, that a nuclear war might be fought without necessarily leading to escalation. On paper at any rate, the outcome was a shift away from deterrence towards possible use of nuclear weapons in war. From the early seventies to the mid-eighties there was much talk of "flexible response," "selected options," "escalation dominance," "decapitation," and even something known as "nuclear shots across the bow."

From at least the time of Korea on, the rationale behind the various American attempts to find ways for using nuclear weapons in war was the considerable gap in conventional forces believed to exist between the US and the USSR. From at least the publication of V. D. Sokolovsky's *Soviet Military Strategy* (1961) on, the standard Soviet response was that the Americans were deluding themselves. Any war between the Superpowers would be full scale from the beginning; it would involve the use of all available nuclear weapons not only at the front but, as Soviet doctrine dictated and Soviet organization implied, in depth as well. Whether, had war broken out, the Soviet threat to escalate would have proved more credible than the American attempt to make first use of nuclear weapons possible by limiting its scope is questionable; but it certainly served the objective—if that, in fact, was its objective—to deter war. One way or another, and in spite of countless crises, forty years of Cold War during which both Superpowers behaved like scorpions in a bottle did not end in a nuclear exchange; by some interpretations, such an exchange had never even been close. However often it was announced that new and much more accurate weapons had brought about the death of MAD, in practice it proved remarkably hard to escape. As Bernard Brodie, in *The Absolute Weapon*, had written as far back as 1946:

> Thus far the chief purpose of a military establishment has been to win wars. From now on, its chief purpose must be to avert them. It can have no other useful purpose.

As additional countries joined the nuclear club—by 2010 there were at least nine, plus any number which were capable of building the bomb had they felt the need to do so—the logic of deterrence began to work for them too. Contrary to the fears expressed by many Western strategists, this turned out to be true regardless of whether they were democratic Americans and West Europeans, or Communist Chinese, or Indians claiming to have inherited Mahatma Gandhi's doctrine of *ahisma* (non-violence), or Pakistanis seeking an "Islamic Bomb," or Jews allegedly possessed by a Holocaust Complex, or paranoid North Koreans. Regardless also whether the nuclear arsenals in question were small or large, primitive or sophisticated, balanced by those of the enemy or not. For a country to wage large scale war against a nuclear enemy without the aid of nuclear weapons was madness. To do so with nuclear weapons, greater madness still.

From the late sixties on, any country in possession of the industrial and technological resources necessary for waging large scale conventional war was also able to build nuclear weapons. Hence, and not surprisingly, there was a growing tendency for such war to be fought solely by, or against, third and fourth rate countries—the most recent cases in point being, as of the time of this writing, Serbia, Afghanistan, Iraq, Libya, and then Syria.

This is not to say that nuclear weapons were capable of deterring *all* sorts of war. Far from it. In particular, the post-1945 have witnessed a great many wars which were not fought by states against each other but inside them, at the hand of non-state actors variously known as militias, guerrillas, and terrorists. Waged not by regular forces invading across some border but at extremely close quarters by people who could barely be distinguished from the surrounding civilian populations, these wars were impervious to nuclear threats. Moreover, as experience in Vietnam, Afghanistan, Iraq, and Afghanistan again, was to show, they could be waged even in the teeth of the most powerful conventional forces in history. Considering that entire continents, and hundreds of millions if not billions of people, came to live under different political regimes as a direct result of such wars, there could be no doubt about their effectiveness; no wonder that they multiplied promiscuously.

Terrorism, guerrilla warfare, and insurgency are nothing new. Throughout history, people too weak to meet their opponents in open battle have resorted to attacking them by stealth, sometimes winning the struggle but more often losing it as ruthless countermeasures, including turning entire districts into deserts, were taken. Nevertheless the first attempts to formulate a guerrilla *theory* had to wait until the second half of the eighteenth century. And even then the term referred not to people's war as we understand it but to what was also known as *Kleinkrieg* or *petite guerre*; meaning the operations of small groups of troops who engaged on the sidelines, so to speak, and were beneath the notice of that novel, mysterious, and August doctrine, strategy.

A coherent theory of guerrilla warfare was, perhaps, put together for the first time by Lawrence of Arabia in *The Seven Pillars of Wisdom*. A typical eccentric—when used to describe the products of Britain's Public School system, the two terms are not as contradictory as one might think at first glance—before 1914 he had studied archaeology at Oxford. During the War he found himself working for British Intelligence in Cairo and it was in this capacity that he was first sent to what is today Saudi Arabia in order to foment a revolt against Ottoman rule. In his book he sought to recapitulate his experiences as one of the leaders of that revolt in 1916–1918. However, whether his contribution to it was really as great as he and his adoring followers tried to claim is a matter of some doubt.

To Lawrence, then, the guerrillas ought to operate "like a cloud of gas." Most of the time they should be inactive and invisible. They should hide in places too remote and inaccessible to be reached by their larger and more cumbersome opponents and rely on dispersion and mobility to escape such punitive expeditions as might be sent against them. Such expeditions, however, might also provide opportunities for action, given that regular forces would inevitably rely on lines of communication which could be subjected to attack. In general, guerrillas ought to avoid head on clashes with the enemy's main body. Instead they were to operate against his flanks, his foraging parties, the garrisons which he put into isolated places and the like; all the while relying on speed and surprise to concentrate their own troops, do their worst, and disappear again before reinforcements could be brought up and retaliatory action taken. Logistically speaking they were to be sustained partly from the countryside and partly by taking arms and equipment away from the enemy, thus making it unnecessary to have permanent, and vulnerable, bases. So far, the theory; however, it should by no means be overlooked that, throughout the revolt, Lawrence and Sharif Hussein received both money and weapons from his British Military Headquarters, Egypt.

As will be evident from the above account, Lawrence was concerned above all with the tactical and operational—assuming the latter term is applicable at all—aspects of guerrilla warfare. In this respect, subsequent authors have added little to his work; after all, there are only so many ways of saying that "when the enemy advances, we retreat." What the other important writer on guerrilla warfare, Mao Tze Dong, added was, first, an analysis of the relationship between the guerrillas and the people at large and, second, his famous "three stage" theory of the way in which the campaign ought to proceed. Dependent as the guerrillas were on the people for shelter and supply, the indispensable condition for obtaining success consisted of gaining the support of that people. Various methods could be used: including propaganda, deliberately provoking the enemy into reprisals, or by main force ("power grows from the barrel of a gun"). If the third method was used, good care should be taken not to allow the guerrillas to become simply a group of marauders. The essential point to grasp—and it is here that Mao made his greatest contribution of all—was that the struggle is primarily *political* in nature.

Drawing on his own experiences as leader of China's civil war Mao, followed by his Vietnamese student Vo Nguyen Giap, believed that the first phase ought to consist of isolated, hit and run attacks against enemy forces with the aim of weakening and demoralizing them. The second would witness the consolidation of guerrilla power in some remote, out-lying, difficult to access, area. From there they would continue their work of propaganda, harassment, and sabotage. Once the enemy had been sufficiently weakened and started to retreat the guerrillas, embarking on the third phase of their campaign, would resort to open warfare. The real trick was to carefully select the moment for this phase to begin. If launched too early it might lead to disaster as a still-powerful enemy hit back. If delayed for too long, the seeming endlessness of the struggle might cause the guerrillas themselves to become demoralized.

To Lawrence, then, guerrilla warfare was mainly another form of military action, one which, to use modern terminology, was "low intensity." To Mao, by contrast, it was above all a question of drawing "the masses" to one's own side and mobilizing them for action. Given that there are clear limits to both indoctrination and force, this in turn meant the implementation of economic and social reforms amounting to revolution or, to call it by another frequently-used name, "people's war." Thus war and politics became inseparable; though in practice Communist-led guerrilla movements in particular always took very good care to ensure that the will of the Party, and not that of the military cadres, should prevail.

The fact that military methods were not so much used as a tool of politics as fused with them made it very hard to fit guerrilla and its smaller parent, terrorism, into the accepted Clausewitizian framework. This is something Mao may have realized. Nor did guerrilla warfare offer nearly as much scope for powerful concentrations of troops and decisive battles against the enemy's main forces as the Prussian writer would have liked to see. As a result, from 1945 on general works which tried to come to grips with the nature of war very often devoted a separate chapter to guerrilla warfare. They almost treated it as if it stood in no relation to anything else.

With the sole exception of Ludendorff, from the 1830s on the most important theoretical framework by far has been the one Clausewitz developed. Moltke and Schlieffen and von Bernhardi and von der Goltz and Foch; Fuller and Liddell Hart (in so far as he accepted that the purpose of war was to serve the political objectives of the state); many of the advocates of limited nuclear war; all these could, and often did, trace their intellectual origins to the great Prussian.

However, by 1990, at the latest, the Clausewitzian framework was beginning to show serious cracks. As has just been said, it proved incapable of incorporating warfare by, or against, non-state actors. To the point that Clausewitz himself, in the five pages he devoted to the subject, treated guerrilla warfare solely as an extension of the struggle between states. At the same time, the question could not be avoided as to whether his insistence on the inherent tendency of war to escalate made him into a reasonable guide to nuclear-armed military establishments, one of whose objectives was deterrence rather than war-fighting.

As long as the Cold War lasted, and with it at least the possibility of large scale conventional hostilities between the Superpowers, these doubts were suppressed. Interpreted as the prophet of limited war, all too often Clausewitz was presented almost as if he were a tweed-clad, slipper-wearing, pipe-smoking, Western analyst. Not accidentally, nobody was more enthusiastic about him than precisely the so-called military reformers who, throughout the nineteen eighties, sought to bring about a revival of "maneuver war" theory. The more countries acquired nuclear weapons, though, the less likely Clausewitz's vision of war was to come true.

Thus it is scant wonder that, as of the beginning of the twenty-first century, military theory seems to be more confused and less coherent than it has been in a long time. Some people, focusing on weapons and organization, still think in terms of nuclear war, conventional war (large or small), civil war, and insurgency/guerrilla warfare/terrorism. Others have constructed their own frames of reference: as, for example, the American analyst Bill Lind did. As Lind sees things, military history since the end of the middle ages has gone through four stages or "generations." The first generation comprised the period from the Battle of Pavia in 1525 to the end of the Napoleonic Wars. Its outstanding characteristic was the slow demise of cavalry in favor of massed infantrymen armed with first pikes, then with both pikes and firearms, and finally with firearms alone. The second generation opened in 1816 and lasted until the last year of World War I. As growing firepower caused the infantrymen to disperse, essentially it relied on long lines of infantrymen supported by artillery of the sort that the British used on the Somme.

The third generation opened in 1917–18 when the Germans pioneered so-called storm troop tactics. Taking the place of the long lines of infantrymen of yore, they relied on cover, dispersion and flexibility to infiltrate through the opposing lines and burst into the enemy's rear. During the 1930s storm troop tactics started to be combined with those new weapon systems, tanks and aircraft, thus adding mobility, range and flexibility. The outcome was the spectacular campaigns that, during the early years of World War II, enabled the Wehrmacht to overrun the continent. However, the evolution of warfare is based on imitation. Starting in late 1942 the Red Army, by combining third generation warfare with vast masses of troops and equipment, increasingly took the initiative. Having done so, within two and a half years it fought its way from Stalingrad to Berlin.

The way Lind sees it, the only Western commander who ever mastered third-generation warfare was George Patton. All others remained stuck in second-generation warfare, a blunt, clumsy instrument that had long outlived its usefulness and only worked because of the overwhelming advantage in firepower they enjoyed over Germany. Meanwhile "the rest" did not stand still. Unable to match the West in terms of technology and firepower, it switched to fourth-generation warfare in the form of terrorism, guerrilla, and insurgency of every kind. The outcome was that, starting at the end of the Korean War—itself, from the end of 1950 on, a classic example of second-generation warfare—and with the sole exception of the 1982 Falkland War and the 1991 Gulf War, Western armies have been going from one defeat to another.

Lind's scheme has been widely adopted. Note, however, that it is based mainly on developments on the tactical and operational levels. It has relatively little to say about strategy, let alone grand strategy and the kind of political, economic, social and cultural factors in which the latter is rooted. In this it differs from some other schemes, including my own which is based on the distinction between "trinitarian" and "non-trinitarian" warfare. Here the assumption is that there are two basic kinds of war, i.e. those in which the distinction between government, armed forces and people is maintained and those in which it is not. The former prevailed in the Hellenistic world, Imperial Rome, and Europe from the end of the Thirty Years War to 1945. The latter ruled most historical times and places including, increasingly, our own.

The two schemes approach the question from two different directions. Nevertheless, they do have some things in common. Both assume, or perhaps one should say, are based on the hope, that deterrence will continue to prevail and that nuclear war will not break out. Both start from the idea that large-scale conventional warfare between major powers has entered its death-throes. Both, though for different reasons and in somewhat different ways, assume that the future will consist of fourth-generation, or non-trinitarian, warfare in which conventional armies with their heavy weapons will be more or less useless.

The most recent development is attempts to combine third- and fourth generation war into something known as "hybrid war." The term started coming into use during the mid-1990s. Since then the Google N-gram graph that shows the frequency with which it is used in print has rocketed into the stratosphere. As the name suggests, hybrid war is supposed to contain elements of both third- and fourth generation, trinitarian- and non-trinitarian warfare. The non-state organizations that wage it rely largely on terrorism, guerrilla tactics, and popular insurgencies. However, they also engage in small-scale conventional warfare. The perfect examples are Hezbollah in 2006 and Daesh (ISIS) in 2014–2015. Neither organization is a state. Neither maintains the usual distinctions between government, armed forces, and people. However, both have enough money, troops, and conventional weapons to do more than wage terrorism and guerrilla alone.

One new form of conflict that remains to be mentioned is cyberwar. Capable of being waged by any kind of organization as well as individuals, it seems to surround all others as the crown of thorns surrounded the head of Christ. Like all other forms of war, cyberwar has its advantages and its disadvantages, its possibilities and its limitations. Given the secrecy in which the field is shrouded, and the limited experience we have with it, the debate about it is only in its infancy. Yet one thing seems clear. In the past, each time advancing technology enabled mankind to move into a new environment—from the land into the surface of the sea, from the surface of the sea into the depths on one hand and the air and outer space on the other—war quickly followed. One could, indeed, argue that it is only when man uses an environment for war that he really comes to dominate it. To that extent, the extension of war into cyberspace appears inevitable. Nor will cyberwarfare always necessarily remain bloodless as has been the case so far.

Some of these forms of war are new, others as old as history. As of the time of this writing, a new and comprehensive theory that will be able to encompass all of them in such a way as to be cumulative, coherent, and clear does not appear to be in sight. Nor does the end of history and the time when wolves will live with sheep. Indeed the author of *that* thesis would be the first to agree that eternal peace might not satisfy those specimens of the human race who are affected by what he calls *megalotimia*, a hungering for great things. As Plato wrote long ago, the only people who will no longer see war are the dead.

Which, of course, is precisely why we need to understand it as best we can.

Bibliography

General

Earle, E. M., ed., *Makers of Modern Strategy*, Princeton, Princeton University Press, 1943.

Howard, M., ed., *The Theory and Practice of War*, Bloomington, Indiana University Press, 1965.

Liddell Hart, B. H., *Strategy*, New York, Praeger, 1954.

Paret, P., ed., *Makers of Modern Strategy from Machiavelli to the Nuclear Age*, Princeton, Princeton University Press, 1986.

Semmel, B., *Marxism and the Science of War*, New York, Oxford University Press, 1981.

Wallach, J. L., *Kriegstheorien, ihre Entwicklung im 19. und 20. Jahrhundert*, Frankfurt am Main, Bernard & Graefe, 1972.

Chapter 1. Chinese Military Thought

Grinter, L. E., "Cultural and Historical Influences on Conflict in Sinic Asia: China, Japan, and Vietnam" in S. J. Blank and others, eds., *Conflict and Culture in History*, Maxwell Air Force Base, Air University Press, 1993, pp. 117–92.

Handel, M., *Masters of War: Sun Tzu, Clausewitz, and Jomini*, London, Cass, 1992.

Sun Pin, *Military Methods*, R. D. Sawyer, trans., Boulder, Westview Press, 1995.

The Seven Military Classics of Ancient China, R. D. Sawyer, trans., Boulder, Westview Press, 1993.

Chapter 2. From Antiquity to the Middle Ages

Aneas Tacticus, *How To Survive Under Siege*, London, Loeb Classical Library, Heinemann, 1948.

Asclepiodotus, *Tactics*, London, Loeb Classical Library, Heinemann, 1948.

Bonet, H., *The Tree of Battles*, Liverpool, Liverpool University Press, 1949.

Contamine, Ph., *War in the Middle Ages*, Oxford, Blackwell, 1984.

Frontinus, Julius Sextus, *Strategamata*, London, Loeb Classical Library, Heinemann, 1950.

Maurice, *Strategikon*, G. T. Dennis trans., Philadelphia, University of Pennsylvania Press, 1984.

Onasander, *The General*, London, Loeb Classical Library, Heinemann, 1948.

Three Byzantine Military Treatises, G. T. Dennis, trans., Dumbarton Oaks Texts, IX, Washington D.C., Dumbarton Oaks, 1985.

Vegetius, Renatus Flavius, *Epitoma Rei Militaris*, N. P. Milner, trans., Liverpool, Liverpool University Press, 1993.

Chapter 3. 1500 to 1763

Barker, T. M., *The Military Intellectual and Battle*, Albany, University of New York Press, 1975.

Frederick the Great on the Art of War, J. Luvaas, ed., New York, Free Press, 1966.

Machiavelli, N., *The Art of War*, in Machiavelli, The Chief Works and Others, A. Gilbert trans., Durham, NC, 1965, vol. 2.

Puységur, J. F. de Chastenet, *L'Art de la Guerre par Principes et Règles*, Paris, Jombert, 1748.

Saxe, M. de. *Reveries or Memoirs upon the Art of War*, Westport, Greenwood, 1971).

Chapter 4. From Guibert to Clausewitz

Von Bülow, A. H. D. von, *The Spirit of the Modern System of War*, London, Egerton, 1806.

Clausewitz, C. von, *On War*, M. Howard and P. Paret, eds., Princeton, Princeton University Press, 1976.

Gat, A., *Clausewitz and the Enlightenment: The Origins of Modern Military Thought*, Oxford, Oxford University Press, 1988.

Handel, M., ed., *Clausewitz and Modern Strategy*, London, Cass, 1986.

Jomini. A. H., *Summary of the Art of War*, New York, 1854.

Paret, P., *Clausewitz and the State*, Princeton, Princeton University Press, 1976.

Chapter 5. The Nineteenth Century

Ardant du Picq, C. J. J. J., *Battle Studies, Ancient and Modern Battle*, New York, MacMillan, 1921.

Bernhardi, Th. von, *Germany and the Next War*, New York, Eron, 1914.

Bloch, J. H., *The Future of War*, Boston, Ginn, 1903.

Foch, F., *De la Conduite de la Guerre*, Paris, Berger-Levrault, 1903.

Goltz, C. von, *The Nation in Arms*, London, Allen, 1913.

Gat, A., *The Development of Military Thought: The Nineteenth Century*, Oxford, Clarendon, 1992.

Hughes, D. M., ed., *Moltke on the Art of War*, Novato, Ca, Presidio Press, 1993.

Schlieffen, A. von, *Cannae*, Berlin, Mittler, 1936.

Chapter 6. War at Sea

Corbett, J., *Some Principles of Maritime Strategy*, New York, AMS, 1972.

Mahan, A. T., *The Influence of Seapower upon History*, Boston, Little Brown, 1940.

Schurman, D. M., *Julian S. Corbett, 1854–1922*, London, Royal Historical Society, 1981.

Gorshkov, S. G., *The Seapower of the State*, Oxford, Pergamon, 1979.

Chapter 7. The Interwar Period

Bialer, U., *The Shadow of the Bomber*, London, Royal Historical Society, 1980.

Douhet, G., *The Command of the Air*, New York, Coward-McCann, 1942.

Fuller, J. F. C., *The Reformation of War*, London, Hutchinson, 1923.

Gat, A., *Fascist and Liberal Visions of War*, Oxford, Oxford University Press, 1989.

Liddell Hart, B. H., *The Defense of Britain*, London, Faber & Faber, 1939.

Liddell Hart, B. H., *The Ghost of Napoleon*, London, Faber & Faber, 1933.

Ludendorff, E., *The Nation at War*, London, Hutchinson, 1937.

Chapter 8. 1945 to the Present

Brodie, B., *The Absolute Weapon*, New York, Columbia University Press, 1946.

Clark, R. A, and Knake, R. K, *Cyber War*, New York, HarperCollins, 2010, pp. 69–102.

Griffith, S. B., *Mao Tse-Tung on Guerrilla Warfare*, New York, Praeger, 1961.

Freedman, L., *The Evolution of Nuclear Strategy*, New York, St. Martin's, 1981.

Kahn, H., *On Thermonuclear War*, Princeton, Princeton University Press, 1960.

Kissinger, H. A., *Nuclear Weapons and Foreign Policy*, New York, Harper & Row, 1957.

Lind, W. S., *The Four Generations of Modern War*, Kouvola, Castalia House, 2014.

Laqueur, W., *The Guerrilla Reader*, New York, New American Library, 1977.

Lawrence, T. E., *Seven Pillars of Wisdom*, New York, Doran, 1927.

Luttwak, E. N., *Strategy: the Logic of War and Peace*, Cambridge, Belknap, 1986.

Orenstein, H. S., *The Evolution of Soviet Operational Art*, 1927–1991, London, Cass, 1995.

Schelling, Th. C., *Arms and Influence*, New Haven, Yale University Press, 1966.

Simpkin, R., *Race to the Swift*, London, Brassey's, 1985.

Till, G., *Maritime Strategy in the Nuclear Age*, London, MacMillan, 1982.

Van Creveld, M. *The Transformation of War*, New York, Free Press, 1991.

Warden, J. A., III, *The Air Campaign, Planning for Combat*, Washington D.C., Air University Press, 1988.

Index

Lightning Source UK Ltd.
Milton Keynes UK
UKHW021949220719
346651UK00007B/21/P